D1624564

knowing where
the fountains are

knowing where the fountains are

STORIES AND STARK REALITIES OF HOMELESS YOUTH

KEVIN CWAYNA, M.D.

DEACONESS PRESS
Minneapolis, MN

Published by Deaconess Press (a service of Fairview Riverside Medical Center, a division of Fairview Hospital and Healthcare Services), 2450 Riverside Avenue South, Minneapolis, MN 55454

Library of Congress Cataloging-in-Publication Data

Cwayna, Kevin.
 Knowing where the fountains are : stories and stark realities of homeless youth / Kevin Cwayna.
  p. cm.
 ISBN 0-925190-71-3 : $16.95
  1. Homeless youth--Minnesota. 2. Homeless youth--Services for-
-Minnesota. 3. Social work with youth--Minnesota. I. Title.
HV4506.M6C88 1993
362.7'4--dc20   93-29236
                                                                  CIP

First printing: November, 1993

Printed in the United States of America
97 96 95 94 93   7 6 5 4 3 2 1

Cover and text design by Tabor Harlow

Publisher's Note: Deaconess Press publishes books and other materials related to the subjects of physical health, mental health, and chemical dependency. Its publications, including *Knowing Where the Fountains Are*, do not necessarily reflect the philosophy of Fairview Hospital and Healthcare Services or their treatment programs.

*this book is dedicated to all of today's homeless youth,
especially those who shared their stories here in the hope
that someone would listen*

CONTENTS

PREFACE

As a child I had what I believed was an unnatural fear of war; it was clear to me that my fear went beyond the acceptable levels established by the older boys in the neighborhood. So, to survive, I suppressed it. As neighborhood kids whose brothers and uncles were fighting in Vietnam or being drafted, the television footage of combat on the nightly news was horrifying. But we had already learned that fear of war was shameful, and death was to be accepted silently.

The Vietnam war was over by the time I was of draft age, but my fear of war and my shame about my fear were still strong. I was apprehensive about the possibility of another war, and I watched the news for clues to this country's possible intervention in trouble spots around the world.

In college, I finally began to relax. To me, college somehow seemed to be a protective buffer. Still, I would pause in front of the memorials to the college students who had been swept off campus and killed in action in the World Wars, but at that time, the threat of being called into warfare like that of Vietnam had begun to feel distant to me. It seemed that the only wars which could affect my life as a young gay man in Chicago were an all-out nuclear war, which of course would not allow for anyone's escape, and the new war against AIDS.

The AIDS epidemic was already being referred to as "the war against AIDS" by the time of my college graduation in 1985, and the description was and is accurate. People I had met were fighting and dying for basic freedoms and human rights; people with HIV, their lovers, and their families were the soldiers. The enemies included the virus itself, societal prejudice, anti-gay and the "you deserved it" religious movements, lawmakers and others who advocated quarantine and mandatory tests, and sometimes even the medical community and social services. They wanted those on the other side dead, isolated, or at least silent. I watched the Army of ACT UP (Aids Coalition to Unleash Power) fight battles against these enemies all over the country. Then, in 1986, during my first year of medical school and at the age of twenty-two, my lover, Eric, told me he had HIV.

I went numb. After fearing war for much of my life, I had been drafted.

For me, this war was not as scary as the kind I had thought about while growing up, but it was just as senseless, infuriating, and sad. And like "conventional" wars, people died brutally. Many died within a short period of time, and they often died alone, silently.

What I saw made me angry, and in spite of my childhood fears about war, I was ready to fight. I understood what was at stake in this war, and I had grown up. Those with HIV did not deserve to be punished or hated—they needed respect and support.

On the home front with Eric, after a time of good health, the war was mostly sad. Instead of gunfire there was the whispered diagnosis, the pain of shingles, the exhaustion of fevers. And all this remained our secret. I would sit in lectures in medical school and listen to the HIV doomsday news, feeling quiet defeat, and every night I would return to where we lived and hold him. Everyone in my class had met Eric, but no one but me knew about his health.

When he died in 1990, at age twenty-eight, I cried hard. But he was one of many I knew who had died, or was dying. The war had been brutal. By the time I finished medical school I had seen too much injustice to go on with my residency. It became clear to me that I was a career military man—I went directly into HIV service and prevention work.

For a time I focused my work on what was then seen as the group at highest risk: gay youth, ages twelve to twenty-one. I worked at the

University of Minnesota's Youth and AIDS Project from 1989 to 1992. But my experiences there led me to believe that there was a high risk group which we were missing—a group which shared a common denominator of risk that went beyond sexual orientation, or even intravenous drug use.

Not all the youths who came through my door with HIV infections were gay boys. In fact, many were straight boys and girls. The risk factor that was common to these HIV-infected youths was not their sexual orientation; it was the experience of being homeless. As I explored this factor, I found that even the gay youths I met who were HIV-infected had been homeless and had lived on the street.

The more I talked with HIV-infected youths, the clearer it became that being homeless was what had put them at risk. They had been forced by a lack of choices to accept exploitation, usually sexual, in exchange for basic necessities like shelter, clothing, friendship, and money. They explained how most youths on the street succumbed to sexual exploitation in some way or another, how even if you tried to stick to panhandling, offers were made daily, and eventually, when you needed the money, food, or shelter badly enough, you would say "yes." The youths I spoke with also explained how drugs were integral to street culture—how drugs opened doors to housing, friendship, and intimacy, how drugs were necessary for pain control, and how those who tried to abstain were excluded.

During the years I worked with HIV-infected youths I saw an emerging pattern. About the time a youth had saved enough money and had the resources to live independently and safely, HIV infection would begin to take its toll. A pneumonia stopped one girl from working; a positive HIV test taken for a military entrance exam closed the doors on one boy. Their stories were tragic, and they infuriated me. Their illness had resulted from homelessness, and now their illness prevented them from leaving the street.

I started asking some questions that went beyond how they contracted HIV and how they were dealing with it. I wanted to know how these youths became homeless, where their families were, and what they encountered in their lives on the streets. And from our social service institutions I wanted to know what, if anything, was being done about the problem. Why were the youths staying on the streets for as long as they did? Who had taken notice that street life was killing them?

I began a three year process of learning about homeless kids. I had worked with street kids at an outreach organization called Lesbian and Gay Youth Together since 1987, and I continued to do so until 1992. But in 1990, I jumped in feet first. I walked with the Street Outreach Workers of youth services in the Twin Cities; I spent many hours in twenty-four-hour coffee shops, where homeless kids without a place to sleep stay up all night. I took special interest in homeless issues at the Youth and AIDS Project. And I met homeless youths everywhere.

They talked freely, and it wasn't long before what they needed most became apparent. Regardless of whose fault it was or who should intervene, homeless youth needed housing—*now*. They needed a safe, decent place where they could sleep, bathe, and store their few things. They needed the protection from violence and a base to center their life that a place of their own could provide. All of them talked about their desire to have a place; many talked about the difficulty of getting a job, registering for school, and staying clean and healthy without a place to live. I began searching for such housing.

Hundreds of phone calls later, I resigned myself to the fact that housing for homeless youth under age eighteen was essentially nonexistent. Public Housing was not accepting applications from youths, and they weren't sure they ever would. Private landlords often had policies about not renting to youths, and community low-income housing projects served only single adults or families. County social services viewed homeless youth as criminals or mentally ill, and never provided housing without some mandatory treatment. Most of the kids I'd met had run from such services. Runaway shelters could only help those who were amenable to family reunification. The situation was dismal.

However, I did discover one sign of hope. There were a few emerging transitional housing programs for homeless youth up to age twenty that assisted them in getting settled in their own apartments and supplied a few months' worth of rent subsidy and some basic services. These programs were different from other youth services in two essential ways.

First, they were respectful of the youths, not viewing them as needing treatment, but as healthy individuals whose behavior was adaptive given their trauma of abuse and homelessness.

Second, and most significantly, they had recognized what was quite evident: in a very real sense, even though many were under eighteen, these youths were no longer children. They would not tolerate being treated like children for the same reasons any adult would not tolerate such treatment. The circumstances of their lives had imposed adult responsibilities and given them adult freedoms at early ages. To ask them to give up their freedoms and responsibilities and become dependent children again (as most government programs do) is to misunderstand their needs and show a lack of respect for who they have become.

Youth responded well to transitional housing programs. Unlike other youth residences, like residential treatment centers, foster homes, and group homes, youths were eager to get into these programs.

Of course, there were problems with the transitional housing programs I investigated, too. Some youths felt isolated in their apartments without friends nearby. It was difficult to find apartments for them, and the goal of having them eventually assume the full rents was sometimes unrealistic. But considering the short amount of time these transitional housing projects had been in existence, they were miles ahead of traditional youth services.

So in 1991, with the assistance of others interested in community service, I founded a small transitional housing project for homeless kids ages sixteen to twenty-one called the Youth Housing Project. I approached the Central Community Housing Trust of Minneapolis, a local non-profit housing developer, and asked to house youths in a few of their units. With their collaboration and a couple of small grants, the Youth Housing Project began. When we first started, we were able to offer subsidized units to five homeless youths. Just as other transitional housing programs had experienced, candidates lined up at our door. All were eager for the chance to live in safety, be independent, and take control of their own futures.

Our program was designed to address the problems other transitional housing programs for youth had faced: the lack of apartments, the affordability of the rents, and the isolation youths had felt. Our rents were lower, our buildings had somewhat greater availability, and youths could live near each other.

These changes proved critical to the success of the youths. Unfortunately, the Youth Housing Project is still overwhelmed with applicants. There are nearly fifteen hundred youths in Minneapolis alone that also need housing, and at the time of this writing we can accommodate only ten at a time. But this isn't a book about transitional housing programs; it is a book which profiles homeless youth.

Most of the youths you will meet in this book came to me through the Youth Housing Project. Their ages range between sixteen and nineteen, but some have been on the street since age eleven. They came on their own or were referred from youth organizations. They sat in my office, usually dirty and worn out, often not having slept for nights. They explained time and time again the barriers they had encountered, the exploitation they had faced. I believe that their stories will give you some idea of their lives, and some insight into what led them to both homelessness and hopelessness.

In this book we will not only listen to these youths speak about how they became homeless and what being homeless is like; we will also listen to them talk about what they need, what they fear, and what they hope for. We will listen to their critiques of the services which have failed them—something that is rarely done by the organizations and institutions which we trust as the "experts" in helping this population. Their assessments are direct and honest, and they can help us reshape tactics and policies to make them more cost efficient as well as more effective in dealing with youth homelessness.

If we, as individuals and as a society, do not change how we respond to these youths and their needs, two things are certain: their numbers will increase, and their plights will worsen. Ultimately, the cost of inaction will be much greater than that of reform.

ACKNOWLEDGMENTS

I am grateful for the assistance provided by the many people who volunteered their information and expertise. I mention only a few: Rex Holtzmer, John Elder, Myra Harris, Jay Wilkensen, the staff at St. Joseph's Home for Children, L.A. Youth Services, San Francisco's Larkin Street Youth Center, the Minnesota AIDS Funding Consortium, and the youths who shared their stories.

INTRODUCTION

"I remember when I had slept in the park one night that summer and had gotten some dust in my mouth. I went to the part of the park where the fountain was and found that there was nothing but a pipe sticking out of the ground. The next nearest public fountain that I could get to without having to get past a rent-a-cop or an 'information desk' was twelve blocks away.

"Twelve blocks is a long way when you've got dust in your mouth, especially when you pass a dozen restaurants on the way. It's a humiliating thing to look up into the window of a cafe, over the crystal and silver, and into the faces of 'upstanding citizens' and know that you could buy an entire meal and all the water you could drink with the change they'll leave on the table. It's equally humiliating when your eyes adjust and you catch your own reflection in the window and realize that the only reason you can't have a drink is because of the way you look: the dirt in your hair, the way you're dressed, and the desperate look in your eyes.

"I found out later that the city had pulled out the fountain in the park due to complaints from the neighborhood. People said, 'it always seems to attract the bums for some reason.'"

—*Kurt, age seventeen*

Homeless youth—youths who are under the age of twenty-one, surviving on their own, and without a safe home environment—exist in nearly every U.S. city and in many rural communities. In larger cities like New York or Los Angeles, homeless youths are highly visible. Their territories are known by street names: Broadway, Larkin Street, Washington Street; or by neighborhood, like Capitol Hill, West Hollywood, and Uptown. Documentaries have explored their lifestyles and cultures, but big city residents have learned to ignore the youths. Their needs are sorely neglected, often overshadowed by our attention to the more threatening issue of drug-related violence, or by the homeless adult or homeless family populations.

In some smaller cities, homeless youth are starting to receive public attention. In cities like Minneapolis there may be drop-in centers, shelters, or outreach efforts. However, in many areas, the presence of homeless youth is not even acknowledged; youths on their own are still believed to be either runaways or juvenile delinquents. The possibility that they have no home to return to is often not considered.

Estimates of the numbers of homeless youth should challenge all municipalities, large and small, to at least examine the phenomenon. Nationwide estimates provided to the U.S. Senate by federally funded youth services range between one hundred thousand on any given night to two million per year. The National Network of Runaway and Youth Services estimates homeless youth to number between one and one point three million per year.

One study estimated that within Los Angeles County alone there were twenty thousand homeless youth in the summer months. For the state of California as a whole, current estimates reach one hundred and thirty thousand. In Chicago, estimates are between ten and twelve thousand, and in the entire State of Illinois, homeless youth are estimated at twenty thousand. In Minneapolis, where most of the youths profiled in this book live, recent estimates of the number of homeless youth range between fifteen hundred and two thousand on any night.

Their presence on our streets suggests a new depth of domestic disarray, both familial and governmental. It also begs a number of questions: Where did these youths come from? Where are the families who are committed by law to provide basic necessities to these youths until the age of consent? Where are the government agencies designed to care for youth without families? In this book, and with the help of the youths themselves, we will find and discuss the answers to these questions.

As we examine the lives of some of these youths through their personal stories, some of our basic assumptions about homelessness and these youths will be called into question. Assumptions about the where these youths come from, about the U.S. Government's provision of care for children without families, about our families, and about our culture. Their stories reflect the unmistakable impression that both parents and public care efforts have retreated from their responsibilities.

At one San Francisco Youth Center, nearly seventy percent of youths' parents contacted replied, "You keep the kid." Thirty-five percent of the homeless youths interviewed in another study no longer knew where their parents could be contacted. Many county and state governments will openly admit that thousands of underage kids they have served are now on the street trying to survive on their own.

According to a survey conducted by Minnesota's Wilder Foundation, most homeless youths have been in and out of at least one governmental care program. The resources we are actually giving our disenfranchised youth are insufficient, and the messages they are left with about life are harsh.

While their mere presence on the street is unsettling, the details of their lives can be horrifying. The accounts you will read about kids eating out of garbage dumpsters, sleeping in abandoned buildings, and selling their bodies may shock you. And there is data to support the fact that their experiences are not all that unusual: the American Medical Association Council on Scientific Affairs, for example, reported in 1989 that the effects of the victimization of homeless youth are comparable to those seen in adolescents in hospital child abuse clinics.

But before their stories will come alive, we must learn to see them in our communities. To the uninformed, homeless youth can be invisible. Like a person's sexual orientation or religious affiliation, a youth's homelessness is often not visibly identifiable. However, once we learn to see them, they will appear. The evidence of their lives will surface all around us, and we will see that we have lived side by side with homeless youth for years.

After reading the stories of these homeless youths, many common sights and experiences may be transformed. Familiar scenes may take on new meaning, and unusual ones may raise new questions. The sight of a young person washing herself or her clothes in a public restroom, for instance, might raise a red flag in your mind. Youths seen leaving or entering an abandoned building might trigger some educated questions. Kids out on the streets in groups or alone long after dark might begin to look like more than rebellious teenagers. In each case, behind both commonplace and more unusual sights, you might see youth trying to survive rather than just causing trouble, trespassing, or loitering.

You may have already encountered homeless youths. You may have been panhandled, solicited, or otherwise confronted by them in a number of ways. You may have let a teenager stay at your house; a friend of your teenage son or daughter. This person may have been someone you never really thought of as homeless, but who actually may have been sleeping at homes of different friends for weeks, or maybe months. Or perhaps you have locked eyes with a kid standing on the street and sensed an undercurrent of need or desperation. You may not have understood his solicitation, but an invitation for interaction may have been made, and his vulnerability displayed.

The notion that homeless youths have rejected mainstream culture and chosen homelessness does have some validity. It is true is that most homeless youths have walked away from something, but it is usually something toxic. Studies repeatedly show that the majority of runaways were mistreated prior to running. They are also much more likely to have been sexually abused as young children than the general population. For the most part, homeless youths have indeed deserted something toxic in their lives, such as abuse, neglect, exploitation, or imprisonment. As such, their homelessness, in many cases, is a choice by default, and for many, their only option. Youths with stable, healthy, loving families may run away, but they more often return home. Homeless youth are different—they are without a home to return to.

On the street, some homeless youths say they have rejected their former world, its culture, and their family. Their dress and behavior may seem strange and confrontational. However, those who project this defiant image are often rewriting their own history to claim control over their lives, and to gain a sense of pride. In reality, behind each defensive facade are stories of brutal battles. Losing battles of kids who have fought to be heard and get their needs met with adults who were unable to hear or care. Battles about safety. Battles about love.

The trauma faced by homeless youth in the forms of disease, exposure, poverty, exploitation, and crime is hard to comprehend, and its preventability compounds the tragedy. We do have the housing space, food, and clothing to care for them until they can care for themselves. We do have the schools and job training to prepare them for independence. But, for many reasons, we have kept it inaccessible, often just out of reach, a few feet from where youths sleep, hungry and cold.

In some ways, our society is ambiguous about homeless youth. We have not decided whether to view homeless youth as deserving of support or deserving of their struggles. Much of this ambiguity stems from our misunderstanding of who they are, where they come from, and how they got in their predicament.

Originally, when services to disenfranchised youth were enacted into law in the 1974 Runaway Youth Act of the Juvenile Justice and Delinquency Prevention Act, all homeless youths were considered runaways, the underlying assumptions being that they left home voluntarily and had somewhere to return to. Family reunification was the goal of all early funded programs.

In 1980, the Runaway Youth Act was renamed the Runaway and Homeless Youth Act, and in 1984, the category of Missing Youth was added to the title. We continue to reclassify and rename disenfranchised youth as our understanding becomes clearer; however, there is nothing to indicate that our understanding has yet progressed beyond rudimentary stages. The stories of the homeless youths in this book may clarify some of our confusions.

Unfortunately, however, our ambiguity also stems from our exasperation around homelessness and around older youth. We are not convinced that homelessness can be solved, nor are we convinced that youths need or want our help. Their stories will also address these beliefs.

Such ambiguities and lack of knowledge have paralyzed our efforts to intervene. But the consequences of our inaction are grim, and will only get worse.

No American would say he is willing to let children die on our own city streets. Yet it is happening every day. Homeless youths are acquiring the HIV virus at alarming rates, and some public health officials have predicted that homeless youth will be part of the third wave of the HIV epidemic in the U.S. In fact, in our large coastal cities it is estimated that nearly one in four homeless youths is infected with HIV. According to current medical knowledge, half of these youths will die in the next ten years.

Homeless youths are also often subject to fatal violence. Others die of drug overdoses, and still others choose suicide. Five thousand teenagers are buried in unmarked graves in the U.S. each year, and one U.S. study presented to the Senate found that after surviving one year on the streets, homeless youths have an additional life expectancy of five to seven years.

The vast majority of these premature deaths are directly related to the perils of homelessness, and are preventable. While we are not willfully murdering these youths, we appear to be willing to kill with neglect.

We do have programs. There are services for youths without families in the form of foster care, group homes, treatment centers, and corrections, and most kids on the street have been in more than one such type of facility. But the services don't work; they are temporary measures at best, they do not prepare kids for living independently, and youths often run from them. Why do youths choose the dangerous streets over these services? Their stories will provide the answers.

The young and homeless may be placed in foster care for their early years. But for most, foster care is only temporary shelter. Many youths run from their foster care, and many arrangements do not work out. And for those youths fortunate enough to form a solid connection with their foster care family, foster care payments to the family often end abruptly when the youth reaches age eighteen. At this time, these kids are expected to live independently, but in reality, they often cannot and do not. Studies of foster care recipients and studies of street kids both indicate that a history of foster care correlates highly with homelessness. A 1991 survey of unaccompanied youth in the Twin Cities area found that thirty-eight percent of the homeless youths had been in foster care. This is not to say that foster care is ineffective as a whole, but it does indicate that in many cases, foster care is not adequate preparation for independent living.

Placements in other institutions, such as group homes, regional treatment centers, and corrections, also correlate with future homelessness. While it is true that the youths placed in such institutions may have lower skill levels and be hampered by other issues that put them at risk for homelessness, it is also true that these placements do very little to prepare the youths for independent living. Some offer crash courses on budgeting, getting a job, or other skills, but others offer nothing of the sort and discharge youths directly to the street at age eighteen. Many focus instead on treatment of the youth's behavioral problems, such as resisting authority, running away, or impulsiveness, although experts on homeless youth believe that many of these behaviors are natural reactions to their histories of abuse, neglect and exploitation.

How did our system get so myopic? How did it become so ineffective at preparing youth for independent adult life? Why are our services most efficient at preparing youth for future dependence on handouts? These are some of the questions this book will address.

In Minnesota, we spend one hundred million dollars annually on foster homes and institutions for our children, and yet they are not effective at even meeting the basic needs of homeless youth. To find out why, we need to listen to the youths themselves. Instead of running to the respected authorities for answers, as we so often do when it comes to social problems here in the U.S., we need to recognize a new authority. Authorities are not always objective. Although they may not be aware of their conflicting motives themselves, authorities have other concerns, including their careers, job security, and respect among their peers. Homeless youths, on the other hand, have only their lives and their survival to be concerned with.

As you read the stories of youths becoming homeless, of kids on the streets, and of street youths trying to get help, a clearer picture will unfold. The causes of youth homelessness will become apparent, the realities of street life will be made vivid, and the ineffectiveness of most governmental and private interventions will become evident.

As we ask the youths what they need, their answers reveal that they are no different than other young adults who want safety, health, a family, and self-reliance. They want to be listened to, treated with respect, and allowed to live independently. They want control over their own lives.

With this in mind, it seems logical to put our resources into assisting older youth to live independently, especially in the face of evidence that our society is finished caring for them as children. It is also logical to try to earn back their respect. They are our children; we share our environment and resources with them. Total loss of respect in a world of limited resources results in war. To earn back their respect, we must assist them with what is important to them. We must give them the chance to take charge of their lives and the opportunity to live independently by safe, legal, healthy means.

Each of the youths you will meet in this book is or has been home-less. I met each of them through one of two places: Lesbian and Gay Youth Together, a weekly support group where I was a adult facilitator from 1987 to 1992, or the Youth Housing Project, a transitional housing project for youth that I co-founded in 1991 with the help of a nonprofit housing developer, the Central Community Housing Trust of Minneapolis. Each youth was asked if they wanted to participate by shar-ing their story only after the primary purpose of our work had been accomplished—i.e., I had found them housing or helped them resolve their crisis—and they had taken at least twenty-four hours to consider whether or not they wanted to participate. Most had gotten to know me over a period of at least a couple of months before I invited them to con-sider sharing their stories in this book. I have changed their names and modified the descriptions of their appearances to protect their anonymity.

No one declined to participate; on the contrary, many youths introduced me to friends who also wanted to tell their stories. All of them talked freely, and I took the liberty of editing out any legally incriminat-ing details. The stories in this book were not chosen because they were the most horrifying or extraordinary. Instead, I chose to present those which were more typical of the experiences of homeless youth. Each story may shock or surprise you nonetheless.

My hope is that this book will point to some positive action for each one of us to take. Some may be in a position to prevent youths from becoming homeless, while others may see ways to assist youths in getting off the streets. Still others may have a means to challenge or reshape cur-rent youth services.

Nationwide reform requires a nationwide awakening, and any awakening requires effort. But the opportunities are everywhere; change is needed in our schools, our local, state, and federal governments, with-in the child care system, and in many of our homes and families.

First, however, we must listen to the youths.

CAUSES

CHANGING REALITIES AND CHANGING PERSPECTIVES

Homelessness has always existed in America, decreasing in times of affluence and increasing in times of economic distress.

The last great surge of homeless prior to the 1980s was during the Great Depression of the 1930s, when estimates of the number of homeless nationwide ranged between two hundred thousand and one and one-half million. However, homelessness during the depression reflected a much more pervasive wave of poverty than that of current times. Bank failures affected nearly everyone, and by 1932, unemployment had reached twenty-five percent. As a result, there was a general sense that poverty was beyond the control of the individual and more a result of macroeconomics. Government reflected this by responding with massive employment programs like the WPA and CCC.

Depression era pictures of homelessness left their mark on America's consciousness. From the depression came the images of the railcar riding vagabond, of the shantytown, of soup and bread lines. From that era too came our awareness of Skid Row neighborhoods and their inhabitants.

As America pulled out of the depression and entered World War

II, the remnants of economic catastrophe converged on Skid Row. Its inhabitants were typically single men, often struggling with alcoholism. They usually worked at day labor jobs and slept in inexpensive flophouses at night. But as bad as their situation was, they had at least makeshift housing, and they often had some form of work; in fact, they were rich by the standards of today's homeless population. And these conditions were generally the case in the postwar years as well.

In a 1958 study conducted in the city of Chicago, it was found that when aged pensioners were excepted, over half of the homeless were employed either full-time (twenty-eight percent) or intermittently part-time (twenty-five percent). Almost all were employed for some period during the preceding year. In contrast, among today's Chicago homeless, only three percent reported having a steady job, and only thirty-nine percent worked for some period during the previous month. In 1993 dollars, the mean annual income of the homeless population studied in 1958 was $1,058, compared to $383 for today's homeless.

By the late 1950s and early 1960s, many Skid Row neighborhoods were being renovated, and the flophouses were closing. Homelessness had declined to the point that researchers predicted it would disappear in the 1970s. However, in the late 1970s and early 1980s, homelessness again gained momentum. Fueled by an increase in housing prices, the destruction of much low-income housing, the deinstitutionalization of the mentally ill, the stagnation of the minimum wage, and the loss of many low-skill jobs to technological advances and foreign markets, many Americans (including families and children) found themselves without housing.

Unlike their Skid Row predecessors, this new homeless population is much more diverse. It includes young adults, persons with mental disorders, parents with children, and children alone. The lifestyles are also different. The old ways of surviving are not available to this homeless population. Cheap housing is gone, as are many of the manual labor jobs that Skid Row inhabitants relied upon. And unlike the national work programs of the 1930s, today's entitlement programs generally do not create jobs, put people back to work, or provide enough income for recipients to secure housing.

A greater percentage of today's homeless are truly without any sort of housing whatsoever. They sleep in the streets, in doorways, in public buildings, or outdoors. More of them panhandle on the streets and look for food in dumpsters. Because permanent housing is often so completely out of reach, emergency shelters become permanent housing to the few who gain access.

The attitudes towards the homeless are also quite different from those of the 1930s. The upper and middle-upper classes fared well in the economic environment which began in the late 1970s and continued throughout the 1980s, while the middle class stagnated and the poor suffered. Taken as a whole, the American consciousness could not then and cannot now resolve this discrepancy. Many of us still hold firm to the belief that the prosperity of some proves the opportunity for prosperity for all.

In the Reagan era, opportunity was available to anyone with determination, or so most of us thought. Tax relief that increasingly subsidized the rich was guarded by those in power as one of the well deserved benefits of prosperity. Attempts to challenge the inequities were diffused by talk of "trickle down economics." The resulting polarization of wealth brought about an attitude that poverty was somehow self-inflicted, and even deserved.

Erosion of government entitlement programs was caused by the lag in cost of living increases in Aid For Dependent Children (AFDC), General Assistance, and other programs. As an example, AFDC benefits in Minnesota had a forty-one percent greater purchasing power in 1974 than in 1991. General Assistance benefits faired similarly. Yet until quite recently, the belief that those who were homeless were too lazy to work and too reliant on government subsidy was predominant. It still persists among certain segments of the American public, although the realities of our economy's fragile nature and its affect on individuals continue to hit home.

Many American families are becoming more aware of how difficult economic self-sufficiency can be because of a common situation: they have children who are now young adults and are struggling to establish their financial independence. This is a phenomenon that is directly related to youth homelessness, and as such is deserving of deeper exploration.

INCREASING DEPENDENCE
ON FAMILY SUBSIDY

B y 1992, the media was announcing that young Americans, on average, were relying on some form of family subsidy until the age of twenty-six. For many young men and women, the subsidy consists of free housing. Most of us know of someone in their mid-twenties who is still living in their parents' home, or who has moved back after trying to live on their own. Suddenly the numbers are too large to simply fault the individuals. America has begun to reluctantly admit that economic self-reliance is almost always difficult for young adults.

Over the past decade, moving out on one's own has become exceedingly difficult. Economists and housing experts know the causes: a static minimum wage and rising unemployment combined with an unprecedented rise in average apartment costs over the past ten years has made available housing unaffordable. And while college used to guarantee a job after graduation, a decrease in white-collar jobs has left many college graduates unemployed, underemployed, or with an income which is inadequate to afford housing.

In the Minneapolis/St. Paul metro area, a region with only minor housing problems compared to many others, twenty-seven and one-half percent of all renters pay more than thirty-five precent of their monthly income for rent, and at least sixteen thousand households pay more than half of their income for rent. For many, finding an affordable unit at all is not possible. By 1989, the demolition of low-income housing had created an unmet demand of thirty-nine thousand affordable housing units.

The phenomenon of young adults relying on their families for basic needs has become so universal that it has been labeled—it is called "the returning to the nest syndrome." But underlying this media label is the assumption that young Americans have a nest to return to, a family to fall back on. Little is said about those young adults without family resources—those whose families have dissolved, or are too poor to offer assistance. How have widespread economic and housing crises affected young Americans without a nest?

For young adults without families, the need for financial support until their mid-twenties is no different. For them, however, a silent corollary of this statistic is much more relevant: until their mid-twenties, young Americans without family support are at high risk for the perils of extreme poverty, such as homelessness. The level of risk is inversely related to the individual's level of education and employment history, but most young people remain vulnerable. While a twenty-six-year-old who has no family resources but does have some post-high school education and employment history may have some chance to achieve self-sufficiency, an eighteen-year-old who hasn't finished high school and has no formal record of employment will almost certainly need some financial support.

Those young Americans without a family nest who do not have the skills or opportunity to achieve self-sufficiency will search for a subsidy from elsewhere. Those with social connections are more likely to find the kind of private and informal subsidy provided by friends. They may stay with peers, or with a series of friends, until they can "get their feet on the ground again." Others, assuming they qualify, will rely on the bare bones public subsidies of General Assistance, Work Readiness, AFDC, or other entitlement programs.

Those youths unable to access these types of subsidy will learn other means of survival. Hungry and homeless, they may learn to panhandle, locate soup kitchens, squat in abandoned buildings, and get food from dumpsters. They may join surrogate families, like gangs or street families, and seek benefits from those connections. Some will survive through the most direct private financial assistance programs available to street kids: prostitution and drug sales. As they do so they will learn about the violence which permeates street life: the violence of crime, the violence of exploitation, the violence of diseases like HIV and TB, and the violence of poverty.

The larger cause of much of the homelessness among today's young Americans is, as it was in the Great Depression, economic in origin. Even those who are educated and skilled do not always find jobs with adequate wages to afford basic housing. Unlike the depression, however, the government has not responded with meaningful and empowering programs to help homeless youth achieve self-sufficiency.

But on an individual level, the dynamics that create homelessness are different. While many families can and will support their children until they can support themselves, there are families that cannot or will not do so. Some families disintegrate before their children are self-sufficient; some drive their children out through abuse or neglect; some find that their limited resources are not enough to care for all their children. From these families come America's homeless youth. And because the belief still persists that if a kid can't make it on his own at age eighteen he just hasn't tried hard enough, these youths are blamed for their homelessness.

The individual causes of homelessness are the ones that you and I can directly address. They are interpersonal and not global, and are about strained relationships and families, lack of support, abuse, abandonment, financial crises, intolerance, and ignorance. These causes include chemical abuse, physical and sexual abuse, serious parent/child conflicts, and poverty.

Many youths run from abuse at home. Some youths are evicted because their parents or guardians can't accept their sexual behavior or their gay or lesbian sexual orientation. Some recent immigrant youths are on the street because their support systems in the U.S. are failing. Other youths appear to want to be on their own. These are the causes we will proceed to examine.

The bottom line cause of homelessness among unaccompanied youth is a premature severance from family support. By definition, homeless youth are surviving on their own without support for basic needs. Severance from a child's family of origin occurs most commonly because of abuse, poverty, or parent/child conflict. However, most severances are complex and contain elements of all three of these. This detachment from the family is premature because the youth have neither the skills nor the opportunities to address their own needs.

Physical (including sexual) abuse, often in combination with adult substance abuse, is believed to be the most common cause of youth homelessness. Homeless youth services in Minneapolis/St. Paul, for example, estimate that over eighty percent of their clients come from abusive homes.

In the following chapter you will meet Sara, a seventeen-year-old homeless youth who describes multiple accounts of familial abuse and alcoholism, and Michelle, a homeless youth who experienced physical and sexual abuse early in life.

When poverty is central, the detachment from family support is more of a deterioration of family than a severance. The stories of Ike and Berhane, told in a later chapter, demonstrate this. When families dissolve, older youth are left with fragile support systems at best; often they must fend for themselves.

In other cases the severance comes about because of a parent/child conflict, often around sexual behavior, sexual orientation, drug use, or cultural conflict. The story of Rick, a gay youth whose experiences are related in the last chapter in this section, exemplifies this situation.

When social services intervene, they often withdraw support before youth can establish their independence and survive. In most cases, county social workers base the aggressiveness of their efforts to provide support on the history of the youth. Many kids who have "failed" the county programs previously are given up on, and outreach efforts are no longer made. Even support for the "successful" foster home child is dropped abruptly on the child's eighteenth birthday. But regardless of the details of the severence, the end result is the same. The adolescent winds up standing alone, without the resources or skills to live independently in a safe, legal manner.

Emotions run deep when the causes are discussed. Court battles may ensue, violence is not uncommon, tears are frequent. The youths blame their families, the parents blame their children, and the social services blame both the parents and the youths. Each camp defends itself against assuming responsibility, and any discussion about it is complicated by this emotional component. But is there any reason to discuss fault at all?

Identifying fault is a waste of energy and does not change the reality that homeless youth exist. In this book, we will avoid the unproductive crossfire of such arguments. However, identifying the causes of homelessness may point to solutions or resources that can effectively address the problem.

Once the causes are identified, we will be better prepared to deal with two important questions: How should social services be designed to address the causes? And should social services take responsibility, or should parents be held accountable? It seems a careful analysis of the causes would not only be helpful, but necessary before resources can be commanded and effective solutions designed. As much as possible, we will proceed with a careful process of analysis, and consider all perspectives.

Causes will be explored without assigning fault. We will take all parties' words face value: those of the youths, their parents, and the people who work with them. We will explore some of the critical motivations and dynamics between the different sides, considering such factors as who has what to lose and who is granted the most credibility. Ultimately, we will listen to the youths, for the youths are the ones who can tell us the most about the realities of their situation.

As we look at the causes more closely, it must be remembered that wherever the problems lie, the youths are the ones who suffer the greatest damage. Parents generally continue their lives, usually with shelter. In spite of the frustrations they may feel, social service workers keep collecting paychecks. The youths are the most vulnerable. They suffer firsthand the consequences of homelessness: the violence, the disease, and the hunger. So when we blame the youths, we blame the victims. And while blaming the victim may be tempting, it is also futile. It does not serve not as a vector towards a solution, but merely as a salve to relieve any other party of responsibility. And after all the arguments are made, the youths are still out on the streets.

In recent years, the national government has changed its position to reflect this. After consistent evidence that at least twenty-five percent of runaway youth had nowhere safe to return to, the U.S. Department of Health and Human Services has adopted a new understanding of homeless youth. Its description of the need for transitional living programs, released in May of 1993, reads: "These young people are often homeless through no fault of their own. The families they can no longer live with are often physically and sexually abusive and involved in drug and alcohol abuse." Certainly the lives of many of the youths in this book are examples of this.

However, while the most common causes of youth homelessness are related to a symptomatically dysfunctional family—one where there is abuse, chemical dependency, or neglect—there are many other reasons for it. Poverty alone can separate a family from their older adolescents; when up against a wall, poor families will stop supporting their older adolescents before they abandon their younger children, and may send them to live with relatives or friends. There are survival incentives for dividing a poor family. Many shelters will take families with small children, but older children are harder to shelter. Some shelters take adults only.

The death or disability of a parent or parents, recent immigration, sexual orientation conflicts, and mental illness are other family stressors that can contribute to youth homelessness. Essentially, any force that weakens a family's infrastructure or serves to detach a child from the family in some way can contribute to youth homelessness.

In this section we will get to know youths who are homeless due to several of the causes listed above: family pathology, poverty, partial family immigration, and an acute family crisis around one youth's gay identity. Because of their relative lack of exposure to family toxins, the youths with more stable families had developed better self-esteem, and their lives on the streets took different courses.

First, however, we will hear the stories of Sara and Michelle, and learn how abuse in their homes resulted in their premature detachment from family support.

CHAPTER

ABUSE

oth sexual and physical abuse are reported by large percentages of youth on the streets. In a 1991 survey conducted by the Wilder Foundation of eighty-one homeless youths in Minnesota, fifty-one percent of the girls and twelve percent of the boys reported having been sexually abused by an adult. Physical abuse was more commonly reported, with sixty-two percent of girls and thirty-four percent of boys reporting such abuse at the hands of an adult. Thirty percent of the respondents reported both sexual and physical abuse.

These numbers are consistent with national data. In a report prepared for the U.S. Senate on the youth served under the Runaway and Homeless Youth Act in 1989, twenty-six percent of homeless youth and twenty-nine percent of runaways reported physical or sexual abuse. Many individual studies confirm that many "runaways" actually leave home because of abuse, and are essentially pushed out by their families.

SARA

"My older brother pinned me to the floor with his knees and kept punching me in the face. My mom stood in the hall watching. In fact, it had been my mom, Dorothy, who had yelled down to the basement for Chris to come up and 'get Sara away from me.'

"Heather, a friend of mine, watched from the bedroom through a door that was cracked open. She didn't know what to do—she stood there silently, looking horrified.

"Chris punched me on the side of the face with a closed fist and yelled, 'you little bitch. Why don't you just obey Mom? You wouldn't get in trouble if you weren't such a snot. You can't hit your mother. I'm teaching you a lesson. Stop crying, you baby. I'm barely touching you, and you're screaming, you fucking baby.' Then my mother said, 'Oh, shut up, Sara, you little baby.'"

I met Sara while working at the Youth Housing Project. After a few months, she decided she wanted to share her story of family abuse, and she began by telling me about one incident in particular when a friend had been over her house. Sara was tall, brunette and "slightly big boned," as they said in her family. It annoyed her that she looked like her mother. She was prettier, though, and she knew it. Her teeth were perfect, and her eyes sparkled. She had done her own makeup for years, and was the consultant in the girls bathroom for those with less skill.

"After Chris and my mother had gone downstairs, I stopped crying and tried to explain to Heather. 'This happens a lot,' I said. 'Mom gets drunk. She picks a fight with me. Mom calls Chris to "protect her" from me. Chris is usually downstairs somewhere, watching TV and drinking. He comes running to Mom's rescue, as if I was this mad dog or something. He grabs me by the hair and pulls me down to the ground and beats me, usually in the face.'

"There was always so much hate in his eyes when he hit me. I'd cry and scream and he would hit and hit. I hate him.

"I got off the bed and looked at my face in the mirror. As usual, there was no obvious damage, other than bloodshot eyes from crying and teased and tangled hair from having my head ground into the carpet. I put in some eyedrops, redid my mascara, and brushed my hair. Then I put on some rouge and looked at Heather again.

"'If things get bad enough,' I explained, 'Mom kicks me out. She's been doing it since I was fourteen. Mom always says, "If you think you know everything and you're so goddamn grown up, maybe you should get out." That's why I went to Dad's last summer. But Dad's new wife is a bitch, and they live in this tiny trailer home, so things didn't work out.

"'While I was with Dad, Mom went to treatment for her drink-ing, so I thought things might be better back here. Of course, nothing changed. Things were good for about a month. Mom was sober then. But pretty soon she was drinking and screaming and kicking me out again.'

"I could tell Heather was shocked by what I'd told her. She was probably thinking, 'How could a parent kick a kid out?' I knew she had a cousin, Scotty, a wild kid from Fridley, Minnesota. He was out of the house by fifteen, but it wasn't because he got kicked out. The story Heather had heard from her mom was that he went to foster care because he was 'too difficult.' They thought he might have mental problems.

"I was smoking one of my mom's cigarettes, blowing the smoke out the open bedroom window so no one would smell it. I'd learned this from Chris. I told Heather, 'I'm embarrassed that you saw the fight, but I'm glad you're here.'

"When she didn't say anything, I went on:

"'Last month when it was real cold I stayed with Cheryl for two nights. Cheryl is great. I tell her everything, but she has four children and they are everywhere in that house. I don't mind sleeping on the sofa, but in the mornings I always feel like I'm in the way. Usually I just sleep in my car when I get kicked out. Last summer I slept outside a few times by Johnson's barn.

"'Sleeping in your car isn't as bad as sleeping in someone else's car or sleeping outside. Outside is the worst. It's loud and scary. I'm telling you, girl, animals come out at night. At night, that field by Johnson's barn is like the Wild Kingdom. I never really fell asleep there. But I only stayed there when Mom had taken my car.

"'If Mom hasn't taken my car, it's just the same damn routine. If it's after a fight, I usually drive around crying until I'm exhausted. Then I try to find a spot to park where no one will find me. And I sleep; sort of. One time, in the middle of the night, Mr. Rabbles—you know, Richard's father—was curious why this old car was in his cul-de-sac. He starts banging on the window. And I jump up to see his scary face pressed against the glass—a real live nightmare. I figured he would get me in some sort of trouble. But I told him I just got tired driving and had to pull over. He didn't recognize me, thank God, and he kind of pretended to believe me while I started up the car and drove out of there fast.'

"Heather laughed—I guess to try to lighten things up, and to hide that she was shocked by what I was telling her. It was hard for her to think that these things were happening in the quiet suburban neighborhood where we lived. But now she'd seen it with her own eyes, and I could tell she was worried for me."

Sara's experience of sleeping in her car isn't uncommon. Most youths on their way to becoming homeless have lived in or slept in cars; often the cars of strangers, cars left open by mistake.

Cars are commonly utilized as shelter after the resource of friends is exhausted. As youths repeatedly find themselves without a place to stay, they work through a temporary shelter continuum. The continuum starts with the homes of friends and relatives, but can move quickly to one's own car, emergency shelters, abandoned buildings (called "squats"), public buildings, strangers' cars, and outdoor locations. The exact sequence and pathway along the continuum depends on many factors, including the youth's preferences, skills, available resources, and gender. Boys are more likely to progress quickly to cars, squatting, and staying outside while girls usually rely on friends for longer periods. In the 1991 Wilder survey of unaccompanied homeless youth, those questioned reported that the most common places to stay included friends' homes (forty-nine percent), shelters (twenty percent), relatives' homes (seventeen percent), and outdoors/vacant buildings/cars (fourteen percent).

There are two pernicious forces in Sara's family which commonly contribute to homelessness of youth: alcoholism and physical abuse. Not surprisingly, the two are often found together, and when they are, they exacerbate each other. The patterns vary, and often involve siblings or extended family, especially when sexual abuse is present. In Sara's family, an alcoholic mother and brother aligned against the daughter and found in her the family scapegoat. The physical abuse was facilitated by the mother, delivered by the brother, and "justified" by Sara's rebelliousness. Without her own family alliances or supportive adults, Sara learned that she was safest when she was out of the house.

Like many other youths, Sara isn't exactly a runaway, nor is she the perfect profile of a "throwaway kid." She is both. Thrown away by her family, Sara is also running away from abuse. And running may be her only alternative; if her home was evaluated by the county on charges of abuse, it is possible she could be returned home with the fault put on her. If interviewed during a sober period, her mother could be evaluated as a responsible parent and could successfully deny everything other than routine disciplinary action when Sara got out of order.

At this point, Sara isn't a street youth, nor is she "seriously" homeless. But she does represent a much larger group of near-homeless adolescents—those who are at great risk of becoming street kids, whose care systems are pulling away. Sara's story is about becoming homeless in one of the most common ways: by severing from an abusive family.

When and if Sara ever lives on the street, some may argue that she chose homelessness. This is, in part, true. She chose to leave rather than risk further abuse. But homelessness is rarely the preferred choice for youth. It is often their only option. Youth can't access adult services because of age restrictions. By contacting the police, homeless youths may risk arrest, imprisonment (in correctional facilities or residential treatment centers), and the wrath of a family which feels it has been humiliated.

Of course, most youths who are on their own are without a high school education, unskilled, unemployed, and broke. As a result, their chances of securing a job or finding housing are slim. What they may find on the street, however, is an opportunity to find a new family, one made up of their peers. It doesn't take long before kids like Sara connect with others who have learned how to survive: namely, the street kids. These are kids who have figured out how to live on their own and get their basic needs met through creative employment—mostly unsafe—and creative housing—mostly illegal.

MICHELLE

Michelle is a seventeen-year-old strikingly attractive Caucasian girl with long thick brown hair, blemish-free skin, a Dentyne smile, and pretty eyes. The world reacts to her sexually, and she has become callous to such flattery as a learned survival response.

I met her while working at the Youth Housing Project, and she agreed to be interviewed for this book. Before we began the interview she told me how the day before, while sitting on a window sill of her new apartment, a man on the street had yelled his phone number to her and pleaded for her to call him. She shouted back, "You're wasting your breath and my time, mister." Yet while this response might lead you to think of Michelle as a hardened and streetwise person, she also exudes naiveté and sensuousness in her persona and dress. She speaks slowly in a low whispering voice and is constantly pulling her hair back and throwing it around like one of the cast members of Charlie's Angels.

What she had to say during her interview may shock you, but it is a familiar story to those who work with homeless youth. She freely discussed being abused, both sexually and otherwise, her involvement in prostitution, and the deterioration of her family. Throughout her story, and from a point very early on in her life, there is evidence of Michelle's battered self-esteem; she accepted the blame for each tragedy, and gravitated towards further abuse:

"I remember walking home from second grade when this kid my age who I had never seen before came up to me and told me he wanted to beat me up. I said 'no.' He said if he could just punch me once he would leave me alone. I let him punch me in the stomach, and it hurt. Then he hit me again and again. I tried to run away, but he chased me and punched me again. Finally, after I was in a ball on the ground crying, he left.

"I never told anyone. For the rest of the year I lived in fear of this boy who would beat me every time he saw me. Afterwards I would just go home and cry in my room. I didn't understand why he wanted to hurt me. I hadn't done nothing to him. I never fought back. I would just fall to the ground crying.

"I guess I never should have let him punch me."

I open Michelle's story with this account because, regardless of the omitted details, this incident is quite revealing. Her reaction to this assault was unlike those of other children, who would likely scream, "I'm telling my mom!" at the onset of such a threat. Michelle's silence is a red flag.

Her resistance to telling anyone of the assault suggests self-blame, protection of the abuser, and an early distrust of the idea that authority would intervene on her behalf. All three of these things are more commonly found in kids who have been physically abused, especially by authority figures, and Michelle was no exception.

Self-blame is a major reason why abuse is underreported. The fact that Michelle accepted at least some of the blame for the beating was evidenced by her statement, "I never should have let him hit me," as if she somehow gave the boy permission to be violent. Also, the extent to which she protected him with her silence accurately suggests past abuse. It indicated a belief that Mom or Dad would not come to her rescue in physical abuse situations. By the time she had reached the second grade, Michelle had ample reason not to trust authority:

"My father was an alcoholic who beat my mother daily. When she was seven months pregnant with me, she divorced him. My mother and I spent the first eight years of my life running from my father. We would move to a new place, change our phone number, and he would find us and beat her. Then we would move again.

"No one could keep him away. Mom would go to the police and to the court, but he always came back. He never hit me, but I would hear him beating my mother, and it *felt* like he was beating me. I would cry and cry. Mom never explained to me why he beat her—she just said he was sick.

"When I was five and six, we lived with my grandmother. My uncle, who was always running from the law, would sometimes live there with us. I don't remember much about the sexual abuse, but I do remember my uncle coming into my bedroom at night. I was scared, and pretended I was sleeping. He would pull down the sheets and touch me all over. It happened a number of times.

"I didn't ever say anything to my mom or grandmother because I didn't want them getting mad at my uncle. I pretty much forgot about the sexual abuse until I was in counseling later, in seventh and ninth grade. But I think Mom suspected something, because one day when I was seven we got our *Time* magazine and there was a naked picture of Adam and Eve on the cover. The cover upset me, so I hid the magazine. Mom asked me lots of questions about why I hid it. All I could say was that I didn't think people should touch each other like that. She asked if anyone had ever touched *me* like that, and I said, 'No.' She asked specifically if my dad had ever touched me like that, and I said he hadn't. I don't think she believed me."

Michelle's strong emotional response to sexual images was suggestive of abuse, and her mother was correct in suspecting abuse given Michelle's behavior. Her confused feelings and ideas about sexuality created other problems for her as well:

"I got a new stepdad when I was in third grade. My mother

married my second grade substitute teacher—they met because I was such a problem child. I was jealous because I had a big crush on him, and was planning to marry him. Most of the times I got in trouble in second grade were just so I could sit by his desk and be close to him.

"When my mother and Donald were dating, they would sit on the couch and kiss in front of me. I wasn't supposed to look, but I couldn't help it. Mom would just say, 'This is what grownups do, dear.' I was very uncomfortable, and I thought it was strange that they kissed so much.

"The first time I ran away was in third grade. My mom and Don had just gotten married, and I felt ignored. I remember thinking I would run away and live with my father in Bloomington. I got as far as my friend's house, two houses down, and her parents called my parents. I was home in a few hours, but I remember liking the attention.

"In fourth grade I was such a disciplinary problem that no one knew what to do with me. I wouldn't listen to any rules from anybody. When school got dull I left, sometimes in the middle of class. Mrs. Rolinsky, my fourth grade teacher, would say, 'excuse me, Michelle, where do you think you're going?' and I would just keep walking. I kept telling my mom I wanted to live with my dad. Eventually, she let me. It had been many years since he beat her, and she saw him treat me real nice when he came by for visits, so I think she thought he'd changed. I also think she was relieved because I was such a problem.

"By age twelve I had bounced back and forth from parent to parent many times. The first few times it was me who wanted to move in with the other parent, but after a while it was my mom and dad who were passing me back and forth after they each had 'had enough.' Both were trying to get rid of me. It seemed like I was never happy where I was living, and I was such a problem child that things never worked out.

"One time I left my dad's because Doris, his wife, beat me. My mom didn't want me living with her, so I ended up at the Bridge, a home for runaway youth. The Bridge is this house in Minneapolis where you can stay for awhile if you're running away. The counselors there were cool, and they didn't try to make you feel bad or anything. Mostly they would just listen.

"I didn't tell them everything, of course—not about the beatings. They would try to get your parents to come down and talk with you and the counselors. It was their goal to get you to return home. But with me they weren't quite sure what to do, because neither of my parents wanted to come to the counseling sessions. Both my mom and dad told the counselors that I couldn't stay with them.

"I felt very sad the whole time I was there. They let me stay there long past the maximum stay, so they could find a place to move me. Finally, on the eleventh day I was there, just as I was packing to go to St. Joseph's Home for Children, my dad showed up. We sat down with the counselor and talked. He apologized for Doris's hitting me and said that he was divorcing her soon. I agreed to follow the basic rules of the house if he kept Doris away from me until the divorce.

"As we drove home I remember wondering why Dad changed his mind, why after eleven days of not wanting me home he suddenly showed up. I never asked him, but I did keep thinking that if he really loved me he would have come to counseling before the eleventh day. I was getting used to this feeling of not being wanted.

"For a few months Dad did a pretty good job of keeping Doris the Monster away from me, but I never heard another word about the divorce. I tried real hard to be in by nine, to do my homework, and not be a total bitch. But not surprisingly, after a few months Doris was hitting me again. I would tell Dad and he would say, 'I'll talk to her about it, Michelle.' Which meant nothing would happen.

"I remember wanting a bruise, wanting to look really beat up. I would go to my room after she had beaten me and look for marks. Sometimes I was red, but it always faded fast. Sometimes I would hit myself in the same places after she hit me to try to make a bruise, but it never worked. Trisha, a friend from school, would bruise if you hugged her too hard. It wasn't fair."

Michelle's story continued with a few more moves between parents before she ran away for good at age fourteen. The episode at the Bridge youth home was an omen; the fact that neither parent was interested in attending family meetings to work on reunification clearly predicted an early detachment from the family for this girl.

In trying to decipher the primary cause of Michelle's eventual homelessness, it is impossible to come up with one clear answer. Certainly her family was unstable and toxic in many ways. Abuse was present on both sides, and neglect seems likely. And certainly Michelle was a difficult child to raise. Her many years as a "difficult child" no doubt eroded her family's support.

All we can say for sure is that in Michelle's and many other cases, homelessness correlates with abuse. Michelle's history of abuse is extensive by any standard. Sexual abuse by an uncle, physical abuse by a stepmother, and violence from outsiders left her without an oasis of safety. Her early exposure to her mother's abuse also shaped her view of parents and other authority figures.

The reasons why abuse is so common among homeless youth are unclear. We must be careful not to assume that because abuse is common, the abuse somehow causes the homelessness. There is no study that explains how abuse causes homelessness.

Reflecting on Michelle's story brings a couple of theories to mind: First, abusive families may be more short-lived than nonabusive families. Such early family deterioration leaves youth without family support at early ages.

The divorce of Michelle's biological parents and the reason behind it appear to have been related to her later abuse, and the split of her natural parents allowed for feelings of less responsibility to their child—the "She's your child, too" phenomenon. However, while such a conclusion may seem logical, I must repeat that I know of no evidence to conclusively prove the theory that abusive families lead to homeless children.

Instead, studies on abuse and their resulting theories focus on the effects of abuse on the victim. It is well documented that victims of abuse, whether sexual or not, suffer from low self-esteem and depression, and are more likely to be violent or abusive towards others. Sexual abuse during childhood is associated with later chemical substance abuse, prostitution, and early pregnancy. An article in a recent issue of the *American Journal of Public Health* went so far as to speculate that early childhood sexual abuse, because of how it may lead victims to risky sexual behaviors later in life, predisposes victims to HIV infection.*

The implication of many of these studies is that as a result of early abuse, the child somehow becomes unmanageable. And it is true that such children are more likely to behave in ways that are not compatible with family life. They may be violent, abuse towards others, angry, or just uncooperative. Who could blame the parents or institutions who must deal with these "damaged" children for giving up? The problem is that in expressing this idea, these studies often blame the child by default, and make no progress towards solving the very real problem of homeless youth.

*(American Journal of Public Health, May 19, 1991, vol. 81, No. 5, p. 572)

CHAPTER

POVERTY

hile the most common causes of youth homelessness are related to a symptomatically dysfunctional family—one where there is abuse, chemical dependency, and/or neglect—there are many other reasons why youths get separated from family support. Poverty is often a major factor in the separation of an older adolescent from his family. Poverty traps families in neighborhoods with more gang activity, drug dealing, and violence. Biological families compete with and often lose to alternative families (gangs) and fast money (drug dealing). And as we've touched on before, when faced with severely limited resources, families will let go of an adolescent to provide for their younger children. This is increasingly true of families from less affluent nations. If they are faced with life-threatening poverty (or political violence) and cannot afford to move the entire family, they send their older adolescents to the U.S., often to live with relatives or friends.

BERHANE

Berhane, a seventeen-year-old refugee boy from Ethiopia, was without shelter again. I had gotten to know him because he had stayed periodically with Ike, another Ethiopian boy who had an apartment through the Youth Housing Project. On many nights, though, Berhane would stay outside. When he came to understand that I would try to help him as I had helped Ike, he began to tell me his story.

Berhane had been in the U.S. for the past six months. He was allowed to enter the country because his older brother, Kiflu, was able to convince immigration that he could care for Berhane. The plan was that Berhane would live with his brother—his legal guardian—go to high school, learn English, secure a job, and then move out on his own.

The reality of the situation turned out to be quite different. Kiflu, while he had essentially saved Berhane's life by getting him out of a war and famine area of Ethiopia, was not equipped to house his brother. Berhane started school immediately, taking English as a Second Language classes, but soon after he moved into a small apartment with Kiflu and his new bride, it was clear that the arrangement was unbearably crowded. Berhane began staying with some new friends he had met through his brother—mostly other refugees from Ethiopia. But despite their hospitality, none of these friends were able to assist him for long. As much of his time and energy was taken up by finding places to stay and moving from one to the next, his school attendance faltered. When he couldn't find someone to stay with, Berhane slept outside with other youth from Ethiopia who had also ended up on the streets.

When I first met Berhane through Ike, he had not been in school for three months. His English was poor, and he had been unable to get a job. He told me how he wanted to go back to school so he could improve his English, but he hadn't found any stable place to live.

I knew I could get Berhane an efficiency unit through the Youth Housing Project within a relatively short time frame, but in the meantime his resources were shrinking. I knew he would need subsidized housing until he was finished with school, but his more urgent need was for emergency shelter. The first day he came to my office, he refused emergency shelter for that night, saying he was "fine for now." The next morning, however, I found him asleep in our office lobby when I walked into work at nine thirty a.m. My appointment with him was not until two o' clock p.m. He had slept outside near an apartment complex, a place he had slept before.

Berhane was clearly without adequate family support. His brother may have saved his life by getting him out of Ethiopia, but the living arrangements he was able to offer were not tolerable. In addition, I suspected from Berhane's story that the decision to move out of his brother's apartment was based on more than a lack of space. (Ethiopian families I had known would frequently live with much less space and privacy than American laws allow—it is not uncommon for four or five people to share a room.) I surmised there had been conflicts over differing personalities, money, or other matters.

I also found it unusual that Berhane was not getting more support from the local Ethiopian community. Ethiopians will readily provide each other with housing and food under normal circumstances, and I was eager to get Berhane connected to more Ethiopian adults. But when we discussed the idea of going to the Ethiopian Community Center, he refused, explaining that the people there were of a different tribe—a tribe with which his tribe was at war.

Berhane had received support from a local immigrant support service, but that service was designed for legal aliens on welfare and was limited in what it could do for non-welfare recipients. In fact, the law stated that it was not to offer any services to non-welfare recipients; they had offered what little help they could to Berhane in spite of that.

Eventually, the Youth Housing Project got Berhane an apartment of his own. He started English as a Second Language classes and soon found a job at the post office. In his case, all that was needed was some temporary assistance until he could establish himself and become self-sufficient. Getting that assistance had been the biggest obstacle.

IKE

Berhane's friend Ike was sixteen years old when I met him, and had been sleeping outdoors or in hallways for the past few weeks. He had been referred to the Youth Housing Project by a neighborhood landlord.

Ike called before coming, and spoke slightly broken English with a polite tone and the careful word choice of a well educated foreigner. He asked me many questions about the Youth Housing Project. Among the first was, "When can I get a place?"

That afternoon he came to my office so we could find him emergency shelter for that night and begin to assess his long-term housing needs. He was a thin, tall, and medium-dark complected boy with short nappy braids, big eyes, and a wide white smile. He wore a Malcolm X t-shirt, black jeans, and a generic red baseball cap. To me he looked like a Benetton model; he had that humane international appearance which that company uses on its billboards and in its magazine ads. I learned that he had been in the U.S. for two years, was a legal alien, and had somehow secured both a social security card and an I-94 card, which he carried around in his pants pocket every day. He did not consider himself African American; he was Ethiopian.

A few months after he had gotten an apartment through the Youth Housing Project, I told him about the book I was writing. He wanted to schedule an interview time immediately. We talked as we sat on the floor of his apartment. He was renting a new efficiency unit with a full kitchen and bathroom for $180 a month. In the corner was a bare mattress that he had gotten from friends, and by the bed was his boom box with cassette tapes neatly piled on top. Above him on the wall were pictures of his girlfriend and his other North African friends who were often visiting. (For the interview, he had asked for privacy. I have since learned that his asking his friends to leave was a sign that he considered the interview a serious matter.) He called his friends his "cousins" or "brothers."

I began by asking Ike, "Where have you lived, and why did you move?"

Ike answered, "My mom, brother, two sisters and I left Ethiopia for Sudan when I was two because of the fighting. My father was in the war, and we never saw him again. He might be dead—I don't know. We left Sudan for Germany when I was four for the same reason: war.

"In Germany, things were peaceful for awhile. We lived in Strasbourg, and I went to public school. But in junior high I experienced some heavy racism. We were the only Ethiopian kids in an all white school. All over Germany, teenagers had formed Hitler youth gangs, like the KKK or the skinheads over here. They were into claiming their superiority and the harassment of minorities. On the TV there were reports of beatings and killings by these gangs.

"One day during the summer I was leaving to go home from playing basketball at the youth center. I had just walked out the front door when these Hitler youth formed a circle around me. I recognized them as guys who were playing basketball next to our game in the gym, but I had thought they'd left a while ago. One guy pushed me from the back, and I turned around, ready to fight, and he said 'auslader 'raus,' which means 'foreigners get out.' Then this big white dude grabbed me from behind and held my arms back while this muscle punk came up to my face and looked at me with hate and anger. He said, 'neger toten,' which means 'die, nigger,' and then he punched me in the gut and kicked me in the groin. The big guy who was holding me dropped me on the ground. While I was on the ground puking, they ran.

"I knew they were serious. There had been killings. I hurt all over with fear. I had to get out of there.

"That night I called my uncle in Minnesota, and he said I could live with him. My mother was torn. All her friends in Germany were saying, 'Don't let Ike move to the U.S. Kids get involved in gangs and they shoot each other over there.' Which I considered ironic, because my life had already been threatened in Germany. But my mom knew these threats were real. She knew how serious I was, she knew I had to get out of Germany, and she knew I was a responsible boy. Finally, she said I could go to Minnesota as long as I stayed in school. I got a student visa for one year and left.

"At first I was doing real well in ninth grade at DeLasalle Catholic School here in Minneapolis. German schools are much harder. Here I was on the honor role and I played basketball. My English was fair when I arrived because of years of English classes in Germany, but when I was immersed in it over here it improved greatly.

"I lived with my uncle for the whole year. He was great. He helped me with English and we talked a lot about life in the U.S. and Germany, and life in general. When I got home from school I had the whole house to myself, and we would eat dinner when he got home at six p.m. He introduced me to lots of Ethiopian families, and I made friends with some other brothers from North Africa who were doing well in the U.S.

"After ninth grade I went home for the summer, but nothing had changed. The racism was just as bad, and while I didn't get beaten or killed, it was probably because I stayed away from gang territory and public places. The Hitler youth were still around town harassing minorities, being more violent than before. Over the past year my mom had become scared of the racism, too, and wanted to leave Germany. I wanted my family to move to the U.S., but my mother had too many debts and my brothers and sisters didn't want to leave their friends. They were all younger and didn't feel the racism as much. I think my mom was too scared to leave, and she was certainly too poor. I wanted to go back to Minneapolis. There was racism in Minneapolis, but nothing like in Strasbourg.

"When I went back to the U.S. I stayed in school for a while, but my second year was different. I couldn't live with my uncle because he was moving to California. I didn't want to move to California, and even if I did, he didn't have room for me there. So I made arrangements to live with a friend named Yohannes and his family who had moved to Minnesota from Nairobi. This arrangement, because she didn't know the people, made my mother very nervous, but she talked with the parents over the phone and decided that she liked them. I think she felt like she couldn't hold me in Germany. They said I could live with them as long as I wanted.

"They lived in South Minneapolis, so I went to Washburn High School. Yohannes and his family were nice and everything, but they were poor and their house was small. I had to sleep in Yohannes's bedroom, which was fine, but we had to share a bathroom with his three sisters. There was some fighting and stuff. Sometimes it seemed like they didn't want me there. Mrs. Goiten was tired a lot, and a few times she got mad when I left dirty clothes on the floor. I never really knew if she wanted me there. Anna, the oldest sister, was in the sixth grade and was getting her periods, so she was always in the bathroom. Once after I knocked on the bathroom door she said to me, 'Ike, we don't really have room for you.' I felt real bad, and I started looking for a place to move to.

"Compared to DeLasalle, the students at Washburn were poor and more wild. There were gangs, fights, and girls with babies. I started smoking pot, which was always available. My motivation got messed up; no one seemed to be serious about school. I got in with a tough crowd and started fucking around.

"At first we would skip class and just drive around during the day to other schools to visit friends. We would meet new people and smoke pot or drink, depending on what we had. By doing this I met a new crowd of Ethiopian brothers. They spoke Eritrean, or Tigrinya, and we could talk about our culture and homeland. They were all from different schools, and some didn't even go to school. Some were homeless, but it didn't seem like it because they always stayed together at one friend's place or another. They became my new family. We hung around all the time and I stopped going to school. Yohannes would hang with us sometimes, but he went to school more often. He kept telling me, 'Ike, you're going to get kicked out of school if you keep skipping.' I didn't really care.

"Around then I met this Ethiopian guy who had a two bedroom apartment and was looking for a roommate. Abebe was about thirty, he was quiet, and he worked a lot. I knew he would think of me as a roommate and not a kid, and I wanted that. Rent was $275 a month. I had to lie to Mrs. Goiten and say that my mom thought it was okay. Mrs. Goiten tried to call my mother to check with her, but she could never get hold of her. She had no choice but to let me move out. I think she was kind of relieved.

"I stayed with Abebe for just barely two months. I stopped going to school, I worked part-time at Taco Hell, and I hung with my friends. Abebe didn't like my friends coming over every day, which I guess I understand. They were kind of wild, but they were my brothers, and I had no one else. The neighbors complained about the noise, and Abebe said I had to leave.

"I told him I had somewhere to live, but I really didn't. I started hanging with my brothers all the time. Usually we would have some-place to crash at some friend's apartment, or we would crash in the hallways of the apartment buildings where lots of our friends lived. Or we would just stay up all night at the Urban Peasant, this all-night cof-fee shop that didn't care if you didn't buy much.

"I met a lot of homeless kids during this time, and some were a little more wild than I was used to. They smoked a lot of pot, some-times stole from cars, a couple of them mugged people a few times, and two guys sold drugs. The drug dealers made some serious money. I was working part-time at Taco Bell making $4.50 an hour, barely affording rent, and I thought about their money every day at work.

"After a while, these two white boys who sold the drugs asked me to help out on some sales, and offered to give me a cut of the prof-its. It was great money. Usually I just did deliveries of marijuana or crack. I felt guilty about the crack. I'd think about the crack babies and I'd see crack addicts walking around all skinny and sweaty, and I felt bad. At night I would think about who I delivered the crack to, and I felt like I hurt them.

"I sold marijuana without guilt. Sure, it can fuck some people up, but not like crack. Getting stoned doesn't make you want to kill anyone—it just makes you want to sit around. I never made the serious money the two white boys made because I didn't get into serious dealing with a pager and phone."

The contrast between Ike's first year at DeLasalle and his second year at Washburn is telltale. At DeLasalle, Ike had stable family support from an uncle who was also Ethiopian and who spoke Eritrean, one of the languages Ike spoke at home. Ike also met a number of North African friends through his uncle, and in them he found additional family. This support was enough for him to achieve academic and athletic success, which further nurtured him throughout the year.

However, during the next year at Washburn, the family Ike was staying with seemed not to have space for him. Their good intentions were sincere, but the family was without the resources to support Ike. Since he was the eldest and the newest addition, Ike felt responsible for the overcrowding and many of the conflicts. The pressure Ike felt was mostly unspoken, although there were exceptions. For instance, when the eldest daughter told him, "we don't really have room for you."

Ike felt challenged to find another family—a new source of connectedness, support, guidance, and love. He found these first in other disenfranchised youths at Washburn, and eventually amongst other disenfranchised North African youths: his "brothers." Both of these surrogate families provided support, but without the resources or knowledge to really help each other get out of the hole of homelessness.

Berhane and Ike were both allowed to live in the U.S. without adequate family support. The official who approved Ike's school visa for his second year exercised questionable judgment at best; at minimum, there should have been periodic verification of family support. The paperwork showed that Ike had a reliable uncle who had supported him successfully for one year, and it was assumed he would support him again, but the facts were different.

School visas supposedly have a built in safety valve to protect against misuse: technically, students are subject to deportation if they stop attending school. The problem in Ike's case was that without real supervision, no one enforced this safety valve. In talking to Ike, I got no indication from him that anyone had ever tried to do so. Four or five months after leaving school, there was still no record of Ike as an illegal alien, something that should have resulted from a report by his school, surrogate family, or uncle.

During the summer he was in the Youth Housing Program, Ike went back to school and straightened out his visa status. But before he came to us, Ike had slipped away from school and away from his surrogate family without much difficulty. Soon afterwards, he had become a homeless street kid.

Immigrant families and individuals often come to this country to escape life-threatening situations. Ike was escaping life-threatening violence in Germany, and Berhane was escaping both violence and famine in Africa. Desperate for safety, Ike got his uncle to vouch for him as his guardian; in Berhane's case, it was his brother.

Many of the youths I met through these boys had left North African war zones or famine areas. Usually they came to stay with family members who had been in the U.S. for a few years. Like many immigrants, these sponsors were poor, and while hopeful, they did not have the resources to support their relative while that person learned English, developed work skills, and got acclimated to a new country.

In working with Ike and others, I met quite a number of young immigrants who had left family members behind and were determined to bring them to the U.S. Within a short period of time after meeting Ike, I was being approached by Berhane and others to declare myself as the guardian of brothers and cousins so that they, too, could come to this country and escape dangerous situations. I could not do so in good conscience, but as I heard the pleadings to save their relatives from famine, violence, and even death, I understood why recent immigrants with scare resources for themselves often agree to sponsor a relative or friend. Unfortunately, the results are fragmented families, fragile support systems, and ultimately, homeless youth.

At the Youth Housing Project, twenty percent of our requests for housing come from recent immigrants. The statistics vary, but in many areas of the country, recent immigrants, both legal and illegal, make up a significant proportion of the homeless youth population. Their ethnicities and cultural backgrounds vary widely from location to location, but their plight is the same.

The Ethiopian background of the boys just profiled is incidental. After all, Ike was actually running from violence in Germany. Berhane and Ike could just as easily have been from Cambodia, Laos, Cuba, Mexico, or any number of countries of origin. Their stories are related here as examples of family fragmentation and youth homelessness related to poverty.

CHAPTER

PARENT/CHILD CONFLICTS

A third category of the causes of youth homelessness consists of acute parent/child conflicts. Disapproval of sexual behavior and orientation, cultural beliefs (a common source of friction between immigrant parents and their Americanized children), behavioral mores, and personal appearance provide the impetus for many serious conflicts between parents and children during adolescence. Sometimes these conflicts end in the youth's exile from the parents' home.

Like those made homeless by poverty, these youths may have been raised within a more stable and supportive environment than those from chronically abusive or chemically dependent families. As a result, youths made homeless by parent/child conflict often have more self-esteem and fewer self-destructive behaviors.

While there may be no long-standing abuse, this third category involves families that often become abusive in response to the parent/child conflict. Typically, these families have exhibited evidence of fragile coping skills before the event. Sometimes there is a history of sporadic abuse, or of other unsettling behaviors. Some of these were present in Rick's family.

I met Rick during my years as a facilitator of a Minneapolis-based organization called Gay and Lesbian Youth Together. He was one of the many youths I came into contact with who had a housing crisis which was directly related to his sexual orientation.

RICK

The last of six children and five years younger than the fifth child, Rick felt like the only child in a family of adults. His parents and siblings seemed big, independent, and busy, and Rick felt somewhat lost. Thin and always slightly below average height, he saw himself as funny looking and hated his thick glasses and big ears.

The other children in his family each moved out soon after their respective eighteenth birthdays, so by age thirteen, Rick was living alone with his mother and father in their modest home in a middle class St. Paul neighborhood.

At school, he had always been studious and quiet. In junior high he never stayed after school for sports or clubs, but preferred instead to go home or to his volunteer job at a retirement home. He liked elderly people; they were gentle and kind, and really appreciated him.

At home, Rick was the invisible child who preferred to stay in his room reading or watching TV. He rarely got into any trouble with his parents. His mother and father had both worked outside the house ever since he could remember, and were usually not home before six.

To his knowledge, none of his brothers or sisters were gay or lesbian, so Rick wasn't sure how his parents would react if they knew about him. He guessed that his mom wouldn't accept him because once, when he and his parents were watching TV, a segment about the Gay Pride Parade came on. It showed two men, one black and one white, kissing. His mother grabbed the remote control and quickly turned the channel. "That's sick," she said, not specifying whether it was the homosexuality or the interracial aspect which upset her. Rick said nothing, not wanting to bring attention to himself, but assumed she was bothered by both.

The Davidsons were a black family with many conservative views and some unusually strict rules. Children were expected to obey their parents without question, and their opinions mattered little. Discussion was rare. Mom was the primary authority figure, and Dad was a silent man whose presence often toned his wife down, but rarely interfered with her authority.

Chores and responsibilities were clearly outlined. The oldest child made dinner every night. Kids and parents ate separately, the kids earlier. (By age thirteen, Rick was the only kid in the house, and by default was in charge of the evening meal Monday through Friday.) Curfew was at nine p.m. Rick described some other unusually strict rules and how they affected his need to explore his dawning sexual orientation:

"I never got permission to sleep over at a friend's house, ever. I couldn't go to the same friend's house two days in a row.

"Gradually I understood why my brothers and sisters had left the house as soon as they were able. There was no physical or sexual abuse—just hypercontrol and lack of support or respect for the kids. Sometimes I felt like the only reason my parents had kids was to do the work around the house.

"As a young child the family rules didn't really bother me, because I didn't know any other way. But by junior high I was carrying around a lot of anger. I was mad about my lack of freedom to socialize and mad about the work I had to do. And to really mess things up, I was realizing I was gay. I really wanted to explore who I was by doing library research, talking to people, and meeting other gay people, but my family rules made this difficult. I grew increasingly resentful.

"Realizing I was gay happened slowly, but soon it became all-consuming. At around nine or ten I knew I was different from most boys in some pretty big ways. I understood girls and their desires, but boys were an intriguing mystery. By age twelve I knew what to call it: gay. I stared at boys all day—my entire fantasy life was around boys. I was in love with one guy after another.

"For a while, in seventh grade, I would tell myself that I was going to go to school the next day, not look at any boys, find a girl-friend, and be straight. Well, the next day I would go to school feeling straight until Jim Corman walked by and then I'd get all those gay feelings again. Of course I was afraid to tell anyone; I could lose friends, get harassed, or even seriously hurt. Fortunately, I didn't suffer from the excessive guilties like most other fag boys. I didn't want to kill myself or anything severe like that. I realized that this was how I was made, and it was good."

Rick, while acknowledging his gay orientation a year or two earlier than the average gay youth, is otherwise a typical example of a gay teen discovering his sexuality. Prepubescent feelings of being different are common, and puberty usually brings intense feelings, both sexual and emotional, towards persons of the same sex.

It is not uncommon for gay youth to be aware of their same sex attractions by age eleven or twelve—the same age that heterosexual kids typically become aware of their sexual orientation. Unfortunately, parents and other authority figures are rarely aware of the facts surrounding sexual orientation. For instance, it is common for parents to believe that children under age eighteen cannot be homosexual. An adolescent who asserts his or her homosexuality at a relatively early age is often seen as rebellious, defiant, hypersexual, or otherwise deviant. This misunderstanding is the basis for much unnecessary pain and conflict, often resulting in either the teen running away or being evicted from the home. People who work with gay and lesbian youth are aware of how common homelessness is within this population; in one study out of Seattle, forty percent of street youth reported being gay or lesbian.

Rick was resourceful and bold in exploring his sexual orientation:

"During the junior high years, I lived in my bedroom. I pretended to do endless homework while I was actually reading everything I could find about what it meant to be gay. Whenever there was anything about gay people on TV, I would watch. At age fifteen, after watching a local TV special on support groups for gay and lesbian teens, I got up the courage to call the local Gay and Lesbian Community Action Council. I remember being so nervous that the phone was shaking in my hand. I asked about support groups, and they referred me to Lesbian and Gay Youth Together (LGYT), a support group run by a local Lutheran pastor.

"A month later, after carefully allibying my way out of the house and navigating the city buses to Minneapolis, I walked into my first meeting of Gay and Lesbian Youth Together. I was shaking, just like I had on the phone. What if I saw someone I knew? What if my mother found out somehow? What if everyone was cold to me, or weird? What did attending this group mean about me?"

Rick's fears were soon relieved. At LGYT, Rick met others who seemed alot like him—others who had grown up lesbian, gay and bisexual. He learned that he was not gay because of some unconscious memory of sexual abuse or seduction, or because of some type of mental disorder. He was gay, which was different from being a transsexual, bisexual, or mentally ill. He listened to the stories of isolation, loneliness and harassment from others like himself. He learned that these problems were the result of homophobia, a widespread fear and hatred of homosexuality. He became aware that he had done nothing to deserve such hatred. He found others to talk to about the isolation and the fear he had lived with, and for the first time he could remember, he didn't feel lonely.

"The group was very important to me. It was the only place where I could really talk about my fears and experiences. I could say something like, 'I'm totally in love with this guy, and I know he would kill me if he ever found out I was gay.' Everyone would say, 'I know what you mean.' At the group I didn't feel shy; instead I felt like my personality was coming out after years of hibernation. I would do anything to get out of the house for those Sunday afternoons.

"At home I hid all my literature on safe sex, coming out, and gay culture in my room. I had a few Equal Times newspapers (a Twin Cites gay and lesbian publication), one soft porno magazine, and one video-tape—no more contraband than any straight boy would have in his room. I never consciously thought my mother would kick me out, but I instinctively didn't trust her reaction, and so I went to every precaution to make sure she never knew. At group every Sunday there was at least one kid who was having problems with being homeless, usually after being kicked out of the house.

"It was sad to watch these kids flounder as they stayed on different couches in different kids' apartments. They would come to group looking like shit because they hadn't slept or showered. Some would stay at tricks' places—adults they would meet in front of the bars each night at closing. Still, the kids in the group were probably luckier than isolated gay youth. We had each other. If someone got kicked out, they could stay with someone they met at group until they could find a roommate and get their own place.

"But some never seemed to make it. I remember Chuck, this flamboyant boy who often cross-dressed. He never seemed to live in one place for more than a week. He was always getting kicked out of some new boyfriend or trick's place and then needing a new place. At group he was either hung over, wired, or sleeping. Everyone said he hustled, and he even admitted it sometimes in group. I saw him on Lasalle Avenue by Loring Park quite often, just standing around. I knew what he was doing. Then one day Chuck was just gone, and no one has heard from him since.

"I was glad I had been exposed to all this when things started happening. After my volunteer job at the nursing home one afternoon in August, I walked into the garage and sensed my mom and dad had had a fight. My dad, who was always putzing around, usually said 'Hi' to me, but this afternoon he just grunted and shook his head. Walking into the house, I found Mom sitting on the steps. She had been crying. I thought to myself, 'They must have had a big fight.' Mom looked at me and said, 'Look in your room.' Then she looked down again. I ran upstairs two steps at a time, scolding myself for keeping anything about being queer in my room, and hoping she didn't find the tape.

"She'd found it. She had dumped out every drawer in my room and found everything; my one magazine, the newspapers, the literature from LGYT. I was horrified at first—I felt cold and sick. Then I was mad. This was my stuff and she had brutalized my entire room.

"Downstairs at the kitchen table, her sitting, me standing in the doorway, the interrogation began.

"'Are you gay?' she asked.

"Briefly, I thought about lying. I thought about saying that the material was for a big research project for school. Too transparent. 'Yes, I suppose I am,' I said.

"She rolled her eyes as if I was being flippant, 'No, you're not. You're only seventeen—you're too young to know. You just think you're gay.'

" I didn't respond.

"'Who got you into all this? Who seduced you?'

"'No one seduced me, Mother. I've known this for a long time.'

"'They have treatment for this. It isn't right, you know.'

"'I don't feel bad about it anymore. There's nothing wrong with it.'

"At first I thought she was listening. I would think about my responses and try to answer honestly. But gradually I realized she was punishing me. Her statements indicated she either hadn't listened or didn't believe me, and her questions were humiliating. At one point she slapped the porno tape on the kitchen table in front of me. She told me she had watched it.

"'Is this the sex you want to do?' she asked. I was humiliated and embarrassed.

"Later in the conversation, after a lecture on relationships where she explained that I must be either the woman or the man, she pressured me to tell her which I was. She wanted to know whether I did the woman role or the man role. I refused to buy into her misconception. I was burning with anger.

"'I am a man, as are both gay men in a relationship,' I said. She paused, then shook her head with disapproval. 'No, you're a boy. A sick, confused boy who needs help.'

"I had never been so mad at her. I looked right into her eyes and told her to fuck off, and then I stormed out of the kitchen.

"The next week was completely silent at our house. Even though I thought her opinion didn't matter to me, it did. I couldn't stand to be in the same room with her, I was so hurt and angry. Dad, as usual, said nothing. I avoided both of them after dinner each night and managed to get out of the house frequently—sometimes with their permission, other times without.

"They never questioned me about where I had been. I think they, too, were avoiding confrontation.

"Unfortunately, that first day I had told her about the group. 'You can't go to that group anymore,' she blurted out one morning at breakfast. 'They're just trying to recruit you. I want you to see a psychologist and a priest.'

"I didn't respond, although I didn't mind going to see a psychologist. I knew that most psychologists were cool about homosexuality, and in these situations they usually ended up counseling the parents on how to be supportive of their gay children. It might even do some good. But the priest thing was stupid, especially given that she was a proclaimed atheist. Her desperation was obvious.

"Over the next few weeks, things got increasingly weird. The tension never seemed to dissipate. She had no boundaries. After my phone calls she'd ask, 'Who was that?' 'How do you know them?' She'd scrutinize my friends whenever she saw them, looking for clues to their sexual orientation. She wouldn't hesitate to ask personal questions about each one of them. 'So, is that your boyfriend?' she once asked in a derogatory tone after meeting one of my friends.

"'As if I would tell you. You'd just harass him if he was,' I said.

"If I left any letters out on my desk, she would read them. When I pressed her for an explanation or let her know I was annoyed, she'd react defiantly and say she had 'a right to know.'

"One night I was on the phone in my room talking to Michael, an older friend at group. I was explaining what a bitch my mother was, and he said I could live with him for awhile. I had no money and I hadn't even finished high school, so I knew it was unrealistic, but we talked about it anyway. After I got off the phone, Mom called me downstairs. 'Who is Michael?' she asked, not looking at me.

"'Michael who?,' I said, not even imagining that she could have listened in and known who I was talking to.

"'Don't mess with me, Rick. I heard your plans to move out.' She continued putting dishes away from the dishwasher and still wouldn't look at me.

"I was enraged. 'You listened to my phone call!'

"'I picked up the line because I needed to call your father. I didn't need to hear much.'

"She was lying—I would have heard a click. She had probably never hung up the phone after she first answered it and said it was for me. I said, 'You read my mail, scrutinize my friends, and listen to my phone calls. You sure are busy, Mom.'

"'I'm just trying to save you,' she protested.

"I was furious. 'I don't need none of your saving, Mom. You're the one who needs help. You're the one who doesn't listen, who doesn't understand anything about gay people, or about me.'

"She immediately glazed over with the most frigid, angry, hateful expression I had ever seen on her face. I think I'd pissed her off more than when I'd said 'Fuck you' that first day she tore through my room.

"After a long pause, she said in a very professional and condescending tone, 'It has become clear that you are too lost in this homosexuality thing. You refuse to get help. You refuse to stop hanging around gay people. You have chosen this deviant, perverted lifestyle, and condemned yourself to loneliness and diseases like AIDS. I can't have this sickness under my roof. I want you out by April first.'

"It was like finally hearing a diagnosis you know you've been at risk for, but never actually expected. I felt numb. But still, with her announcement came some relief. Maybe I could really get out of the hell I was living in.

"I decided to make this easy on myself. I would leave on April first and not talk to her again. 'Fine,' I said, and I walked upstairs.

"The next two weeks brought more silence between me and my parents. My mom never tried to apologize or explain again why she was kicking me out. She was silent on the issue.

"I had stopped cooking them dinner. I would take food upstairs to my bedroom and eat while I talked on the phone to friends from Lesbian and Gay Youth Together. Mom never bothered me about dinner. I think she doubted I would actually leave. Dad was his usual absent silent self.

"On April first, I took what I could fit into two suitcases and moved out. I lived with Michael and his roommate Rob at first. They were eighteen and nineteen. But it was a one bedroom apartment, and I felt I was imposing by sleeping on the sofa every night. Still, I was determined not to drop out of school, and I got on the city bus in Uptown Minneapolis at six a.m. to make it to my high school in St. Paul by seven fifteen.

"One day after school I went to the bank to get the last of my savings out and found that my mother had closed the account. It was one of those parent custodial accounts, and she had withdrawn the entire $300 I had earned the past summer mowing lawns and baby-sitting. My mother was continuing her harassment of me even now that I was out of her house. I asked around, but everyone thought that there was nothing I could legally do to get the money back."

After the first week, Rick could tell that Michael and Rob were getting frustrated with having him in their space, and it was straining Rick's friendship with Michael. By the second week on his own, he moved in with other friends from LGYT. At seventeen, there was no way for him to get an apartment or sign a lease, and he had no savings, employment, or rental history. Fortunately, he was very likable and had many friends who were out on their own. He continued to rely on their generosity, even though most of them had little more than he did.

Two months later, after finishing high school, Rick got a job at a museum through a temp agency, and it opened up into a permanent full-time position. He started saving for an apartment. By his eighteenth birthday, after bouncing around from friend's place to friend's place, he had his own apartment and a full-time job with benefits. And while he had foregone his college education, he was self-sufficient. At the time of this writing he is nineteen and continues to work at the museum full-time.

While lucky in some respects, especially with his employment situation, Rick's success was somewhat predictable. He had a number of advantages over other youth who find themselves without housing. Many of his advantages stemmed from the stability of his family of origin. Rick was from a family with some history of neglect, but without a history of major abuse or dysfunction. He had had a stable childhood within a relatively supportive family. As a result, he was a kid with an intact sense of self-esteem, an internal locus of control, the ability to trust others, and the ability to ask for assistance.

His assuredness around his sexuality and his accurate conclusion that it was his mother and not himself who needed help show a significant strength of ego in a challenging situation. This strength gave him a resiliency to trauma, and especially to internalizing blame for it. This kind of strength can translate into a guard against becoming depressed and nonfunctional, as so many homeless youth do. It is common for homeless kids with less self-esteem to refer to themselves as "fuck-ups" and to feel helpless to improve their situations. Rick, on the other hand, quickly saw his eviction from home for what it was—an irrational reaction from an angry and hurt woman who misunderstood her son's sexuality.

Rick always felt he had some control over the course of his life. He had confidence that he personally could determine the path his life would take, and as a result (and with the help of supportive friends) was able to see that his basic needs were met. Rick believed that his high school diploma was still obtainable; he believed that he could achieve financial self-sufficiency. These beliefs helped him take concrete and sustained steps towards these goals.

Unfortunately, many homeless youths do not believe that their lives are in their control. They suffer from the opposite belief pattern from Rick's self-determination, sometimes called "learned helplessness." This is the inability to make sustained efforts to change a situation because of an underlying belief (often substantiated by the youth's experiences) that control of the situation is external. Learned helplessness often results in paralyzing depression and hopelessness.

Rick had a number of other qualities that helped him: he trusted others, he was able to ask for assistance, he was likable, and he was sincere. These qualities (particularly his abilities to trust and ask for help) are believed by some professionals to be the natural outcome of a consistent and stable family life. They are often not present in other homeless kids who have experienced early abandonment, abuse, or institutionalization. And if it was there to begin with, trust of others is quickly lost by any kid who lives on the streets long enough to feel the exploitation of street survival.

Finally, moreso than Sara, Michelle, Berhane, or Ike, Rick was well connected within a supportive network of other stable youth living on their own. These friends served as a surrogate family and provided resources he needed for stability. Also, unlike the friends made by Ike, Rick's friends had apartments and jobs.

We began this section by exploring youth homelessness due to abuse and chemical dependency through Sara's and Michelle's stories. Next, we looked at how poverty can play a large part in youth homelessness through Ike and Berhane's eyes. Finally, Rick's story offered an example of how a parent/child conflict can result in homelessness.

Now that we know some of the whys behind the problem, we will listen to youth as they discuss the realities of homelessness and describe life on the streets.

REALITIES

Today, in alleys in Rio de Janeiro, street kids are gathered at gunpoint and shot execution style by death squads. These death squads are hired by local merchants.

For $33 per head, store owners routinely invest in "cleaning" the streets of young criminals. After execution, the bodies of these children and adolescents might be tossed into the garbage if they are not simply left where they fell. There is no great effort at covering up these murders, because the chance of a conviction is slight. With over one hundred and eighty such death squads identified in Rio alone and six thousand murders committed in the past four years, prosecutors are overwhelmed. Add to those numbers the fact that many of the members of the death squads are soldiers and law officers, and you get some idea of the depth of the problem.

In Brazil, public sentiment for the country's two hundred thousand street kids is mixed. While there are more than six hundred services to assist street kids in greater Rio, segments of the public, angry at the high crime rate, blame government neglect and support private solutions to crime. The death squads are the most extreme example, but the belief in taking justice into one's own hands is widespread. Samuel Correia, a host of a local provigilante radio show entitled *Crime Patrol*, became so popular that he was elected to the State Legislature.

The crime that the Brazilian youth are usually guilty of, the one that can get their name on a death squad list, is stealing. However, with poor to nonexistent earning potential and few resources, their alternatives to stealing are few. In effect, they are being killed for trying to survive. Furthermore, the number of executions indicates that the employment of death squads is meant to more than just deter other youth from stealing. The strategy is to eradicate the problem through mass extermination.

To the best of my knowledge, street youths in the U.S. have not been systematically eliminated by execution. However, the effect of many of our policies and reactions, particularly when they concern inner city street kids, has been just short of execution. Not admitted to most shelters for the homeless because of their age, street youths are regularly evicted out of their illegal shelters and provided no alternatives. Their possessions, including their food, money, and clothing, are often confiscated by authorities.

The violence they suffer on the streets includes beatings, rape, and murder. In the U.S., five thousand youths are buried in unmarked graves each year. On the streets they are at extremely high risk of contracting a number of diseases, including HIV, which can lead to AIDS. In fact, youth services in San Francisco and Los Angeles report that in our large coastal cities, up to one in four street kids has acquired HIV infection, resulting in an average life expectancy of less than ten years.

Unwanted pregnancies are common, and prenatal care is rare. Frostbite and gangrene can result from exposure to the elements.

No, there are no known death squad executions of street kids in the U.S. Instead we allow our homeless population to die from neglect.

In our culture, we rely on the experts to inform us. Unfortunately, when it comes to homeless youth, the experts we put our trust in are themselves uninformed. In Minnesota, for example, unaccompanied youth have been uncounted for years because they are not allowed in most emergency shelters. The "experts," usually those who work for the government in social services, rely heavily on emergency shelter survey data. From this data Minnesotans hear facts about the adult homeless population, or about women with children, but hear very little about homeless youth. Since no one was counting the unaccompanied youths, no one knew the extent of youth homelessness in Minnesota.

The one exception has been the relatively few agencies and private organizations which serve youth. In America's cities, the people who work at local drop-in centers for street kids know that there are more homeless youths than the "experts" realize. Services for runaway youth have more adolescents requesting help every year, and outreach workers who deal with them testify that the city streets are swarming with youths.

THE SURVEY

Finally, in 1991, in response to requests from youth service providers, the Wilder Research Foundation embarked on the first survey of the homeless youth population in Minneapolis/St. Paul. Youth workers from a number of different agencies volunteered to survey youths on one night, citywide. With a colleague from the Youth and AIDS Project, I surveyed Hennepin Avenue, a busy central street in Downtown Minneapolis. We asked each kid we found hanging around a few questions to see if they were indeed homeless. Every one of the youths we approached qualified. They were happy to sit down with us in return for five dollars, and for half an hour they shared their private lives.

One youth I remember, a seventeen-year-old African American girl, had just left work at her full-time job as an actress at the Children's Theater Company. She and her eighteen-year-old boyfriend were waiting for a bus that they thought they probably missed. She explained how she couldn't go home because of her mother and stepfather's alcoholism and abuse. She had stayed with friends many times, but couldn't continue to do so. The Children's Theater Company couldn't pay their youth staff because they were classified as students, and her work at the theater didn't leave her time for another job. As a result, she couldn't afford a place to stay, so she stayed with her eighteen-year-old boyfriend wherever they could find a bed. Sometimes they stayed at his family's house; other times with friends. Lately they had been staying at a squat on the west bank of the Mississippi River.

Three other youth I interviewed shared similar stories about abuse, exploitation, and homelessness. Two were working, but like the first girl, they didn't make enough money for shelter.

My colleague and I interviewed the youths while sitting on the sidewalk on the corner of Seventh Street and Hennepin Avenue. The stream of youths who walked up and down Hennepin Avenue was almost constant. We were the only two advocates interviewing youths on Hennepin Avenue, and from what we saw it appeared that we missed many youths eligible for the survey. The entire staff of interviewers surveyed eighty-one youths throughout the metropolitan area that night, and the number was limited to that only because of a lack of greater resources.

The results of that Wilder survey indicated that homeless youth in the Minneapolis/St. Paul metro area share many traits with homeless youth from other U.S. cities. Like their counterparts nationwide, roughly fifty percent reported either physical violence or sexual abuse at home. Approximately sixty percent reported previous out of home placement, such as foster care, residential treatment, or corrections. The majority reported leaving home more than once, and seventy-five percent reported that they came from the local area. The survey simply confirmed that the details of the problem in Minneapolis/St. Paul are no different from those of other areas of the country.

The reality in the U.S. is that if a youth finds himself alone on the street at sixteen, fourteen or even eleven, regardless of the reasons, the burden of survival may well fall on him. Families and government agencies can and do skirt responsibility.

State and county agencies may be meant, in theory, to care for all youth without families, but in reality this is rarely the case. The social services placement programs in many areas (including Hennepin County in Minnesota) usually do not place youths who are sixteen or over. Such older youths are considered to be out of their realm of responsibility. As overburdened and underfunded as many county youth social services are, younger kids are the priority. (Even among the younger adolescents, however, there are some that are written off by county agencies. These are the kids who have "failed out" or run from placements so frequently that county social services considers them "lost.")

Families that evict older youths are not held accountable. Often no one takes responsibility for providing a safety net of basic needs should these kids be hungry, cold, or ill. Parents, motivated by the potential loss of their Aid For Dependent Children (AFDC) payments, may order authorities to charge their evicted children with running away. However, none of the legal advocates for homeless youth has heard of a homeless kid who has charged her parents with neglecting to provide support.

The reason is that the legal world of adults does not exist for homeless kids. They look to other means of meeting their most basic needs, and the following chapters will illustrate the most common of them.

CHAPTER

SURVIVAL STRATEGIES

To survive, street youth find each other, stick together, and form "families." In fact, street kids in the U.S. have their own culture. They share common experiences, beliefs, language, and even traditions. Their culture includes being familiar with the intricacies of various means of street survival: prostitution, panhandling, stealing, squatting, and working the social service system as best they can.

Their cultural beliefs involve a distrust of adults, a strong attachment to their street families, and irreverence towards the law. Their common experiences typically include sexual and other types of abuse, family severance, and multiple placements in foster care, group homes, and other settings.

The culture of street kids is one focused on day to day survival. The need for food, shelter, and safety are daily priorities, and securing such necessities can be all-consuming. The means by which these youth get their needs met is parasitic in nature; not out of malice, but by necessity. Most of what they use has either been discarded by others or given to them as charity, and although many say that they would prefer to earn their living, homeless youth are ill equipped to do so.

There are few legal means by which homeless youth can earn enough money to meet basic needs. Greater than seventy-five percent of them do not have a high school diploma or the equivalent G.E.D., so their employment possibilities are greatly limited. Furthermore, their lives on the street without home phones or bathing and laundry facilities make it difficult to succeed in getting an interview, let alone keep a job.

In spite of these challenges, nearly thirty percent of the youth interviewed in the Wilder survey had found some temporary employment (without health care benefits, of course), and eighty percent were enrolled in some school program. However, most were not attending school, and those who did find work were working just to survive.

Street kids are extremely poor, both in resources and marketable skills. Their access to money, basic necessities, or, for that matter, anything of value, has been severed along with their relationship to their parents, families, and communities. The resources which they see around them each day, such as public and private buildings, automobiles, and restaurants, are out of reach. Even forms of shelter which are empty or discarded, like vacant buildings, are not available; our government spends money to prevent homeless youth from using these resources.

Street culture is at once both fragmented and unifying. It is fragmented in the sense that most youths only participate in certain aspects of the culture—usually depending on their main hustles. One girl may make enough money through prostitution to avoid squatting and panhandling, while another boy may be skilled at panhandling and thereby avoid eating out of dumpsters. Some may find havens in gangs, while others may be victimized by them. However, the common ground for all street youth is their focus on daily survival; they share a language which describes basic needs, and they share a history of living from crisis to crisis, of dealing with social service agencies, and of family severance.

Street youths typically come from various mainstream cultures, but their street lives are foreign to most of us. Street life is characterized by violence, exploitation, day to day survival, and marginalization. Still, a homeless kid may find a family, and will certainly learn various hustles as means of surviving. She will learn a new set of behavioral mores as well as practical considerations, such as where to sleep and where to get food and money. She will also learn how to get cigarettes, beer, pot, and other substances to medicate her feelings.

For the most part, however, the values of street culture deviate only slightly from our values. Street youth generally avoid violence, preferring to ask for money rather than take it by force. They will usually salvage items from the garbage before they steal new ones, and will sleep in unheated vacant buildings before they break into homes in search of shelter. In choosing these means of meeting survival needs, they may simply be choosing the easiest ones, or be trying to avoid legal altercations. They may be trying to stay invisible. But no matter what their motivation is, their decisions reflect the fact that street kids still to some extent respect or fear our definition of personal property.

The meager resources they do manage to acquire are almost always low-quality, and can often cause physical harm. Living in a place without heat is not only uncomfortable, but in Minnesota and other northern cities, it is dangerous. Eating out of dumpsters is not only unpleasant, it is a health hazard. Acquiring enough money through panhandling to feed oneself or one's baby is often a lengthy and tiring process, and is in some ways less efficient than taking money or food by force.

Eventually, as street youth become further alienated from our culture, they will begin to feel justified in taking what they need directly. From what we know about street youth in other countries, it is clear that after ties with mainstream culture have been deeply severed, survival through more drastic means arises. Theft and violence become the norm.

In the eyes of a homeless kid anywhere in the world, life on the street is a life on the outside. Much of the day is spent standing on the edges of a more prosperous world, looking in. What a homeless youth sees is that there are those who seemingly have everything, and then there are those like himself who are struggling. And while he can see prosperity all day, feel it as a car brushes against him on the street or a shopping bag rubs against his leg on the mall escalator, he may not share in it. Somewhere, somehow, his access to these things has been cut off.

One component of life that loses focus on the street is the future. With the demand for a street kid's attention constantly on day to day survival needs, the foreseeable future shrinks from a span of years to a few days. Dreams of professions or status that may have been realistic when the youth was still attached to school and family fade, and are replaced by hopelessness.

Sometimes the hopelessness is disguised by dreams of wealth and prestige, as seen in the film *Paris is Burning*, which depicted the "fashion balls" put on by homeless youths in New York City. Other times the hopelessness is expressed by anger towards those in better situations. Often it surfaces as depression.

Each of the homeless kids I interviewed for this section talks of lost dreams. Each one grieves their losses in different ways, yet holds onto new, if more modest, hopes. These hopes invariably have to do with getting off the street.

DAVID

David Aaron Harris, a nineteen-year-old Caucasian hard rocker with a black concert t-shirt, long blond hair, profuse acne, and bad teeth, walked into my office at the Youth Housing Project with an older man. He was kicking David out because he claimed that after giving him a place to stay, David "sat on his ass for five weeks." The older man looked about forty-five, was dressed in a conservative business suit that couldn't hide his substantial girth, and spoke in a loud agitated tone:

"He hasn't found a job or gone to school—he's just eating all my food."

David sat across from me, rolling his eyes as if to say, "this guy is lying."

I asked to speak to David alone. Jerry, the man he was with, was resistant. He said, "I wanted to be here to make sure he doesn't lie to you."

"I appreciate that," I said, "and I'll get back to you with anything I need your input on." Jerry reluctantly agreed to wait in the lobby.

Once we were alone, David told me he had met Jerry by hitchhiking, which was one of his hustles. "The guy bought my sob story and invited me to live with him until I could get my feet on the ground," he said. I was suspicious that Jerry had approached him for sex, but I decided to let David tell me at his own speed.

When David moved in, he promised Jerry that he would get a job and find another place to stay as soon as possible, and from what he told me, it sounded like he had demonstrated initiative in doing these things. In the five weeks he had gotten a job in the stockroom of a department store, but had quit after he was docked a day's pay for something that seemed unfair to him. A legal adult, he had applied for and received food stamps, had applied and been rejected at the Job Corps, and had applied at a temporary employment agency.

"Jerry expected me to be on my feet in a week—he's this high-powered banker who thinks the world is just full of opportunity for everybody. He doesn't realize that my opportunities are limited to those businesses and organizations who will take a chance on a kid who looks punk and has no local work history. There aren't very many of those. Even the fucking Job Corps, part of the U.S. Government designed to give underprivileged kids a chance, rejected me."

"Why did they reject you?" I asked.

"They dicked me around and kept delaying everything. Finally they said something about my warrants in Seattle and Portland, and I knew they were saying 'no.'"

Warrants are common among those who have lived on the street. I didn't ask about them because I didn't want to put him in a defensive situation where he would be protesting his innocence at this early point in the interview.

His history was notable for his extensive time on the street. David said he was nineteen and had been on the streets since he got kicked out of the house at age eleven. He had been through a few foster home placements and had spent two years in juvenile corrections, but had otherwise lived on the streets. The reasons he gave for his foster home not working out were typical:

"They wanted me to be part of this really intimate family where I told them everything and we hugged a lot and all this bullshit. I wasn't into it. I didn't trust them, and I didn't want to be close to them. I felt uncomfortable and I knew I was a disappointment to them. I started being bad again—getting into fights, skipping school, the usual. Eventually I ran."

David had lived in Portland, Seattle, Anchorage, Madison, and now Minneapolis. When I asked why he came to Minneapolis, he described some trouble he had gotten into in Oregon for supposedly selling someone else's pot. He claimed he hadn't done it.

"Then the guy who owned the pot turned the whole street world against me. Everyone thought I was a backstabber, and no one would help me anymore. I knew I had to go. The other cities I thought about, Milwaukee and Chicago, are too brutal and violent these days. So I hitchhiked to Minneapolis."

David had slept outside quite often, but he usually found some abandoned building and made it his home for awhile.

"The other street kids will tell you where it's cool to squat. Usually, after they've seen you around for awhile, they will bring you to their squat. If I'm totally alone I look for the squatter's symbol—a lightning bolt through a circle. That means that people have squatted there and it's cool. I try not to sleep in a building alone, though. It's too scary and dangerous. That's when you get rolled, beat up, or raped."

Despite his extensive pattern of vagrancy and his long history of street survival, David talked a lot about wanting to "settle down and make something of myself." I needed more details before I could determine whether this was a hustle to get my cooperation or if his desires were authentic.

When I pressed for details, he said, "I want to have my own stuff, my own key to my own apartment where I can go and crash whenever I want. I want to get my G.E.D. and work so I can pay my own way. I'm sick of owing people everything and borrowing everything. I want to find a girlfriend and settle down."

David's experiences on the streets explained the origin of these desires. "On the street," he said, "everyone steals your shit. You get rolled all the time, which is crazy because you usually don't have anything. If I work for awhile, for a temporary service or something, I don't have anywhere to keep the money. I don't have anywhere to put anything I buy. I used to drag a lot of shit around, but there's no point unless you can see that you'll have a place soon. Which I usually can't see.

"I can always get money from people," he went on. "Panhandling is one of my hustles. But people fucking harass you. They'll pretend to give you money and then scream 'get a job, asshole!' or something really nice like that. Other people act real scared, as if you're going to kill them or something.

"Seems like everyone thinks you're going to buy crack or drugs with the money. I tell them what I need the money for. First I ask for money for food; after that, cigarettes; and after that, beer. I don't often get to the beer part, but I'll tell people. I'll say I need some money for food, or ask, 'Can I have some money so I can get fucking wasted and forget about my life for awhile?' People pay. If you're clever you get more money. My famous line is, 'I need some money because my hamster needs an abortion bad.' Then I look down real sad and say in a soft voice, 'she was raped.'

"I think it's great when people offer to buy you a meal. They'll walk with you to some restaurant or food stand and watch you eat like a horse. Then you don't have to worry about food for awhile. Otherwise it can take you hours to get enough change to buy anything. I meet a lot of people this way.

"This is my life: looking for food, cigarettes, beer and shelter, and I'm very tired of it."

I had noticed that David was wearing a cap turned to the side, usually a gang symbol. I asked him, "What gangs have you hung with?"

"I got my name—HiCee—from the Crips, a gang I hung with in Seattle. I was down with them, which meant I was their friend, although I never officially joined. The Crips' color is blue, and they live for their color. I know some Crips that have died for their color, protecting the name."

I knew that anyone who was "down with" a gang was usually a full member, so I was suspicious that he was minimizing his gang affiliation.

"Are you associated with a gang now?" I asked.

"No, it's too violent. In Seattle there wasn't anybody against the Crips—at least not up on Capitol Hill where I hung. But in other areas the gang wars are tough."

"How about here in Minneapolis?"

"I don't know the scene; I've purposely stayed away. I'd rather survive."

"Why are they violent, do you think?" I knew if he was a gang member, he would be likely to rationalize or minimize the violence.

"They're protecting their brothers. But some of them just like to fight. It's a penis thing—you know, macho image. They've tried to start fights with me for no reason. One dude will come up to me and say something like, 'Yo, dude, you're real ugly. You want to make something of it, bitch?' I usually just say 'no' and hope they leave me alone. If you want to start a fight with a Crip, you call him a Crab. With a Blood, you call him a slug."

I continued to verify his knowledge base. "What do they use to fight?"

"They'll use whatever's around. If there's a stick, they'll use it. If there's a rock, they'll pick it up. If there's a glass window, they'll put you through it. If there's any way to draw blood, they'll do it."

His words matched what I had heard from other street kids. "So they'll kill you if they can?"

"Sure," he said matter-of-factly. His casual attitude towards gang killings made me suspect he had seen a few.

Without making him feel as if he was being interrogated, I wanted to know why he had gotten involved with the Crips. "What do the gangs provide?"

"People think they're organized crime, but the gangs aren't that organized. The mob is organized crime; the purpose of gangs is more around fighting, brotherhood, support, and territory. There are benefits to being down with them. They'll get you stoned if you want. You can hang in their house or cave or wherever they are and listen to music. You can sleep at their pad. They'll protect you if they see you getting harassed.

"I was down with the Crips in Seattle, but if I went up to one in Portland or Minneapolis and said, 'Yo, Crip, what's up, bro?,' they'd say, 'Who you trying to be, punk?' and I'd likely get beat. In other words, you're only down with the Crips you know—others won't acknowledge your connection. If you're an actual member, then your membership transfers, but I was never an official Crip.

"I was hardly ever down with any gangs except the Crips in Seattle. Instead I've got street brothers, people I can trust and with whom I share everything. I've got street brothers in cities all over. It usually takes some event to find out if someone is a brother. Like in Madison, this guy asked me to hold his pot until he came back. Well, he didn't come back until the next day, and I was still hanging around and I hadn't touched his stuff. He was shocked that I was still there. He said, 'Man, I thought you would have split and sold it. You're cool; you're a brother.' So from that day on we were together and shared everything. It's easier to survive when you're together.

"I have street dads, too. Those are usually people who've taught you a new hustle. One dad taught me how to steal speakers and stereos from cars and where to sell them. I'd get a buck apiece for speakers and five or so for a car stereo. A pair of speakers is a pack of cigarettes. A stereo is a meal. Sometimes you can sell them at pawn shops, but usually only those rundown cluttered-looking ones. If you walk in and there is shit piled everywhere, they'll probably buy your stuff."

David also admitted to drug dealing. He sold pot for dealers in many cities at a one hundred percent markup, and the profits sustained him for much of his street life.

I wanted to assess his HIV risk and his involvement with prostitution, so I asked, "How many people who pick you up for hitchhiking want something in return?" He knew immediately what I was getting at, and smiled.

"About ninety percent, I'd say. There are a lot of gay men out there who will pay you for sex and will pick you up hoping you will take money for sex. I've never done it. I'm straight, and I've never needed the money that badly. I always tell them right away that I'm straight and I don't do sex with guys—which are two different things."

I was doubtful that he had never turned tricks, so I let him know that I could see why he would have. "It seems like an easy way to earn money even if you are straight."

"It is. Most of the guys I know have done it, but not me. That's what Jerry, the guy I've been staying with, wanted. He told me I was the kind of boy he liked. A boy with long blond hair and a muscular body."

"But he let you stay with him even though you wouldn't do anything?"

"Yeah; I think he was hoping I would change my mind. After a few weeks, when he realized I wasn't going to put out, he wanted me to bring other street boys home for him. He told me he would pay me twenty dollars for each boy I brought home. I told him I wouldn't do it. It's all part of the reason he wants me out now."

"Have you been in similar situations with men before?"

"Yes, many times. Usually they kind of fall in love with me and let me stay, but then after a while, when they realize I'm not going to have sex with them, they end up hating me. So I move on. They usually don't fuck with me, because I'm pretty tough and I scare them."

While you may find David's story incredible or shocking, it is actually very characteristic of those related by street youths. David shares a number of experiences with other youths who have lived on the streets for awhile, including his own repertoire of acquired hustles, his desire to get off the streets, his association with gangs, and his continued movement from place to place and city to city. Unlike many others, however, David is still alive after being on the streets for six years (during the ages of eleven through nineteen, minus two years spent in a foster home and corrections facilities). The reasons for his survival include his keen survival instinct, his avoidance of violence, the skills he has learned, and most importantly, his luck.

Like the average American, David has had six or seven career changes in his lifetime. But unlike others whose lives follow a more conventional path, David started his at age eleven. His careers, defined as such because they are means of survival, included stealing, drug dealing, panhandling, squatting, and social networking. His valuable skill of being able to connect with adults and tap their sympathy allowed him some flexibility in his hustles. For those who can overlook his personal hygiene and who have something he wants, he is charming. (This quality must not be mistaken for trust or intimacy, neither of which David readily offers.)

His lack of trust and ability to get close to people were offered as his explanation for his short stay in foster care, when he said, "I didn't trust them and I didn't want to get close to them."

Rex Holtzmer, a Unit Supervisor in the Children's and Family Services Department of Minnesota's Hennepin County, recognizes this as a major barrier: "Foster care families are looking for kids they can include in their family. The problem is that many youths needing foster care either never had family intimacy, or have been hurt by it. The result is that often these kids don't bond, they don't trust—they are well defended emotional islands."

And yet David appeared to be able to form street family relationships with other youths, calling them "street brothers" or "street dads." In David's case, as in those of most street kids, the explanation is multifold. First, relationships with street dads are survival relationships, and do not necessarily involve emotional intimacy. Second, street family relationships are with peers—homeless youths who are of the same age or only slightly older. Adults are generally seen as abusers, but other kids are more often viewed as allies. Third, other street youths are recognized as insiders, having gone through similar experiences; they are not part of the mainstream culture, unlike foster families.

This dichotomy of trust within the street world and mistrust of anything institutional is commonly seen in the emotional framework of street kids, and it must be understood by any service organization interested in reaching these youths. Having something that street kids need for survival is not enough to entice their participation. Agencies proposing to provide services to street youth need to appear to be youth dominated, nonauthoritarian, and noninstitutional. Otherwise, they will not be trusted. This lesson was learned long ago by two types of successful street "outreach" groups—namely, gangs and pimps.

The very qualities that make street gangs distasteful to mainstream America are the qualities that attract street youth. Gangs appear to be youth-dominated and noninstitutional, and offer homeless kids what they need: a family, some basic resources, and employment training—albeit for illegal employment. David saw in the Crips both a source of protection and basic needs, and a family.

The Crips didn't require ID, appointments, forms, and a processing time before food and shelter were provided. Once he was "down with" the Crips, David had immediate access to food, shelter, and company. Fortunately, David had an aversion to violence. He joined a gang only when there wasn't any ongoing warfare ("In Seattle their wasn't anybody against the Crips..."). Other street youths are less discriminating or less fortunate, and get caught in the crossfire of gang warfare.

Typical of youth who have been on the street for years, David had a desire to settle down, get his own place, and find a job and a relationship. He was tired of the violence and the crisis survival lifestyle of the streets. Unfortunately, the excitement of a crisis lifestyle can be an addiction; about the time that coming clean becomes desirable, the lifestyle has become second nature and is difficult to leave.

David had learned to cope with stress by fleeing. This habit, an adaptive behavior on the streets, will probably continue to impede his ability to obtain self-sufficiency. My own experience with him bore this out. During the interview, David seemed very excited about the possibility of acquiring his own apartment through the Youth Housing Project. I explained how the damage deposit and the first few months rent would be covered. But three days after the interview, David had, I heard from another youths, fled out of state.

The difficulty of leaving street life can surface in many forms. Youths may be so used to being with other kids that they are uncomfortable when alone. This can result in them having trouble acting autonomously in any situation, from employment to apartment living. When youths are involved in gangs, often the gangs will not permit them to leave.

We will explore gangs, chemical abuse, street families, internal emotional barriers, and other obstacles to self-sufficiency more thoroughly in a later chapter. Right now we will turn to another reality of street life—sexual exploitation and the high risk of HIV infection.

CHAPTER

SEXUAL EXPLOITATION AND HIV

hile David, the youth profiled in the last chapter, consistently denied sexual exploitation, his story shows how opportunities for it are everywhere. Unfortunately, many other youths are not as resistant as David.

In light of this fact, it is not surprising that the Center for Disease Control in Atlanta reports that homeless youth appear to be a new wave of the HIV epidemic. This is confirmed by interviews at the Youth Housing Project; a number of the youths we talk with are infected with HIV and know it. Others have not been tested. All are at high risk.

Even without AIDS, being young and homeless in a U.S. city is dangerous. Emergency room statistics indicate that trauma amongst homeless youth is common: gunshot wounds, stabbings, and beatings are facts of street life. In Washington, D.C., the county hospital reports that amputation after frostbite and the resulting gangrene is a frequent procedure on the homeless.

But when combined with the threat of sexually transmitted diseases, the plight of homeless youth becomes much worse. County or private STD clinics, such as the Red Door Clinic in Minnesota's Hennepin County, verify that STDs and their complications, such as

Pelvic Inflammatory Disease and infertility, are not unusual amongst homeless girls. And with the advent of AIDS, homelessness is often fatal. A study conducted in San Francisco in 1991 found that twenty percent of the street youths were infected with HIV. Given what we know about AIDS in 1993, the medical community projects that all who do not die prematurely from other causes will certainly die from the disease.

How do these youths acquire the HIV virus? Adolescents and young adults who are without a home on the streets of U.S. cities are both vulnerable and highly exploitable. Within a short period of time on the street, most youths are offered money for sex. Protection is rarely discussed, and when it is, youths are offered additional money for unprotected sex. These kids quickly learn that their bodies can earn them cash, and in a world where relatively small amounts of cash can be lifesaving and nearly impossible to come by, this knowledge, if not used immediately, is stored away.

Sexual exploitation comes in many forms. The familiar form of prostitution, with a male pimp and female prostitutes, is only one of them, but there are many others. Most youths are approached by the johns directly, on the street, in public shopping centers, or at a park. Also, prostitution among homeless youth is an equally viable source of income for boys and girls. Oral sex by men on boys can earn them thirty dollars. Anal sex can be more lucrative. Finally, sexual exploitation often comes in the form of "survival prostitution"—sex in return for basic needs such as clothing, food, shelter, and friendship. Many youth like David who are befriended by an adult soon learn that the arrangement, whether it provides shelter, food, or friendship, comes with a price. When the adult is HIV-infected, this price can be their life.

While they are often bombarded with AIDS prevention messages, and even though most actually have the knowledge to prevent contracting HIV, the infection rate among homeless youth is high. After listening to their stories, however, it is understandable why prevention efforts are lost on them. For the youth on the street who is living hour by hour, struggling to meet the daily needs of shelter, food, and clothing, information about a disease that may kill them in ten years is irrelevant. This is especially true when the information comes from someone who is ignoring their basic needs of today.

For street youth, the future is already bleak, and thinking about it is a source of great anxiety. Many homeless youths don't believe they ever will become adults. Others find refuge in unrealistic fantasies about stardom and wealth. Very few regard the future as something to be protected and nurtured every day.

MICHAEL

Michael, a nineteen-year-old boy, has been hustling on the streets of Minneapolis for years. With long dark hair, pale skin, and a thin boyish body, Michael had a number of regular customers, and all of them were men. He learned to prostitute, his main hustle, at age sixteen, when, after a series of evictions and out of home placements, he found himself alone on the streets. Within a few hours a man had offered him a ride and solicited him for oral sex. He made thirty dollars in ten minutes.

Sitting across from me in my office, he told me about his experiences.

"Under the bridge at Fourteenth and Lasalle in Minneapolis is a good place to stand, for two reasons. First, there's a big heating vent that's part of the inside bridge wall. Heat blows out of the Hyatt hotel or the restaurant nearby—we never figured out where from exactly, but it didn't matter. It's warm, and we were often cold. Also, the traffic is good; lots of action. Closer to Loring Park, like on Willow Street, it's too obvious. The police know what's up. All the pedestrians know. And I'm a straight boy. I don't want everyone knowing that I'm working. Girls don't like boys that work."

"How do you let the men know that you're working?" I asked.

"Well, first you scan the cars for men driving alone. Then you look at them in their cars to see if they're looking at you. If they are looking, then you keep looking right into their eyes real hard, tilting your head and turning around if you have to. If they slow down and turn around some corner, then you know.

"My friend Donnella, the drag queen, would always chase the cars down the street. We'd say, 'Donnella girl, don't. You look too damn desperate.' She'd say, 'I *am* desperate, girls, and so are you or you wouldn't be out here.' And she'd go running down the street after some car like somehow if she caught it, it would be filled with money.

"Anyway, I never wanted to leave the heat, so I would always wait by the vent. Usually if the car slows down, then it drives around again and pulls up to you and the driver rolls down the window. Billy, my hustler friend, told me that if the guy is a cop, and you ask him, he has to tell you. So my first question after they ask 'Do you want a ride?' is always, 'Are you a cop?' No one has ever said yes, and I've never been arrested.

"Even though I stand by the big heat vent, the warmth of a nice car feels better, and if they seem at least sort of normal I get in. I'm not scared because I can always protect myself. If it feels weird I just get out of the car wherever. I've never had to fight anyone. The worst thing that ever happened was I got stranded in some place with farms around it. It took me a day to walk back to the city. So now I always ask where they live. If they say someplace out of Minneapolis, I tell them we got to stay in Minneapolis. I know everywhere in Minneapolis and I can get back to my friends from any corner."

Most street kids pride themselves on their ability to survive and handle dangerous situations. Michael talked at length about how he could sense danger and was careful to avoid it. If and when they start to trust the person they're talking to, however, their defenses often retreat, and their stories change.

"It's easiest when they want to stay in the car, like if they don't have a place to go because their families are at home, or they have to go back to work or something. But I'll go back home with someone if they live in Minneapolis. Sometimes I've been in some pretty nice homes in some pretty fancy neighborhoods.

"Usually they want to suck me off. I tell them I don't get hard, which is the truth, but they don't care. They just want to beat off while they suck me. I just sit there while they do their business, looking around the room or the car wondering what I could steal. After they're done they usually drive me back and then pay me. Thirty bucks is the going rate, and everyone seems to know it. They know that if they don't pay me I won't let them do it again, so they usually pay up."

Michael was open about certain details of his hustling, but he remained guarded about the more humiliating, traumatic, or emotional experiences. And although he didn't discuss the other sexual behaviors he engaged in for money, I believed he engaged in anal sex without protection. I say this because Michael denied intravenous drug use but was HIV-infected. Anal sex is a likely means of HIV transmission.

He found out he was infected after two years on the street, when he tried to enlist in the Army at age eighteen. The day he got his rejection note with his test results he went on a drinking binge, then vandalized his parents' suburban home. Three days later he arrived at a drop-in center for homeless youth and told one of the workers there about his infection. I was working on a research and service project for HIV-infected youth at the time, and I was called in to meet him.

Michael was a manic yet entertaining kid, with a capacity for great outbursts of anger and dangerous drinking binges. After his initial reaction, he had accepted his infection without surprise, explaining, "My life is just one shitty thing after another." Over the following two years, however, he suffered many bouts of paralyzing hopelessness.

Yet, with much personal attention from workers at a number of agencies, Michael earned his G.E.D., got himself out of prostitution, and began working. I found Michael his own apartment through the Youth Housing Project, and for a few months he worked steadily and paid his rent in full, but then he was hospitalized with three different HIV-related complications.

As of this writing, Michael occasionally takes his AZT, but more often than not he skips it. He was recently referred to a psychiatrist for depression.

There is no good data on the prevalence of HIV among the Minneapolis/St. Paul street youth population. What we do know is that many of the HIV-infected youth under age twenty-one have been or are now homeless. Their stories reveal that the risk for HIV is incredibly high while surviving on the streets. Not only are kids regularly approached for sex within hours of being on the streets; intravenous drug use is also common. And in our larger coastal cities, the extent of the problem is considerably greater.

In coastal cities, data indicates that a large percentage of street kids are HIV-infected. In Los Angeles, for instance, information gathered by youth services indicates that eighty percent of street youth have been involved in prostitution, forty percent have used injection drugs, and depending on their ages, between fifteen and twenty-five percent are HIV-infected. In San Francisco, the Larkin Street Youth Center estimates that one in four street kids is HIV-infected. And there is no reason to believe that the infection rate among street kids will not continue to escalate.

The AIDS prevention messages we send are ineffective, particularly in the case of homeless youth. Close examination of them reveals that they are often either unrealistic or dangerously misleading. Take, for example, the message, "wait until you are married to have sex." This message not only assumes that everyone at risk is heterosexual, it also assumes that marriage is always possible, affordable, and unfailingly leads to monogamy. Many homeless youths see marriage as a conventional mainstream cultural practice that is not available for them. Furthermore, many of them have witnessed abuse within the context of their parents' marriages, and others have experienced the effects of serious family dysfunction.

As a result, this message about marriage as a means of AIDS prevention carries within it a number of alienating submessages for these youths. It does not acknowledge that dysfunctions within a marriage are possible; the abuse or infidelity these youths have seen within marriages, they are being told, simply does not happen. It does not acknowledge the existence of those for whom marriage is illegal or out of reach—gay or lesbian youth, the socially disenfranchised, the destitute. Considering what these youths have seen and experienced, this assertion of the sanctity of marriage as a preventative health measure only alienates them from mainstream culture further.

The messages delivered espousing monogamy as the answer to HIV are also empty and destructive, particularly to street kids. There are two which are commonly heard. The first, that one should have sex only in a monogamous relationship, is up for a multitude of interpretations depending on your definition of monogamy. The second, that protection is not necessary within a monogamous relationship where both partners have tested negative for HIV, is a setup for failure.

The perceived glowing sanctity of monogamy has overshadowed the need to be clear and specific with our messages. For instance, those who work with homeless adolescents understand that to them, monogamy often means having one partner at a time. Although they may be streetwise, few of these youths are jaded enough to see a brief sexual relationship for what it is—they commit to monogamy with the frequency and predictability of the seasons.

Just as society teaches, many of them believe that love is forever. In their minds, a promise of monogamy from a partner (or a john, for that matter) gives them permission to be sexual. Sometimes they take that promise of monogamy as permission to engage in unsafe sex. In my interviews with youths, they invariably list a multitude of relationships that had the best intentions of monogamy. They frequently even believe that their johns love them, are devoted to them, and are monogamous. Even otherwise cynical adolescents approach relationships with the plan to stay together forever. On one level, at least, this is not surprising; it is how they have been taught to justify any sexual contact.

The second monogamy message, that protection is not necessary if both partners are monogamous and test negative for the HIV virus, can result in disaster. While the message is factually correct, if one partner is sexually active outside the relationship without the other's knowledge, the implications are explosive.

I have worked with a number of youths who were not using protection with their partner after both tested negative, only to have them discover that their partner had not been monogamous since. The result is that not one, but two youths become infected with HIV.

The bottom line is that youth need to learn to maintain both open communication and caution in their relationships. Nonmonogamous partners often keep silent because confession could mean consequences they would like to escape: a return to protection for six months, going through retesting for HIV, or, as in many cases, the end of the relationship.

I cite these ineffective AIDS prevention messages as preface to stories and analysis to come. In the stories of the youths that follow, we will look at the other messages they hear about sex, behavior, education, and employment. One example is the often heard exclamation, "Get a job!" Obviously, this is not realistic for youths without an address, an alarm clock, or a shower. We will see that like most AIDS prevention messages, these other messages are equally absurd, and often indicate a lack of understanding of the lives and situations of street kids. Instead of helping, the messages reveal mainstream society's ignorance, and serve to further alienate homeless youth.

MICHELLE

In order to examine a different path of sexual exploitation, we return now to Michelle, who in an earlier chapter told us how her relationship with her family deteriorated. As you'll remember, she spent the first six years of her life with her mother, running from her physically abusive father. During this period she was sexually abused by an uncle and suffered recurring beatings by a neighborhood boy. As time went on, her mother let her stay with her father, and eventually she found herself passed back and forth from mother to father with great frequency. She felt unloved, and began to try running away.

Michelle told me the following story as we sat in the efficiency apartment that she had gotten through the Youth Housing Project, and which she had been living in and renting for the past six months.

"Eventually I ran away and stayed with friends—first Julie, then Trisha (the girl I was jealous of because she bruises easily), and then Rachel. Usually their parents would be nervous about pissing off my dad by hiding me, so I couldn't stay too long. Then I met Kathy.

"She was eighteen, had a two-year-old boy named Scooter, had lived on the street for years, and had gotten her own place through a transitional living program for homeless youth nearly a year before. All her clothes were black, her hair was dyed jet black, her nose was pierced, and she smoked filterless cigarettes. She said she used to do cocaine, crack, and other drugs, and she used to be a prostitute, but she was all through with that bullshit. She was on Aid For Dependent Children (AFDC) and her two bedroom apartment was in South Minneapolis. Kathy seemed real together, and when I told her my situation she said I could live with her if I worked to help pay rent.

I was sixteen and already had a job at Burger Slop making nearly-five dollars an hour. I knew I didn't have to go to school after sixteen. It all seemed so perfect, so I moved in. I loved Scooter, which was a good thing because I baby-sat with him nearly constantly after I moved in. I guess Kathy thought that with me around to take care of Scooter she could go party like she used to. One time she was gone for four days. I had to miss work to take care of Scooter, and I lost my job. I called her friends looking for her, and they told me she was probably on one of her crack binges. This was a bit of a shock to me, because I had believed her when she told me she quit.

"Scooter and I went to my friend's house for a while because I was so angry, and when we got home I found that Kathy had come back and taken her TV, stereo, VCR, and most of my clothes. I figured she was selling them for more money for crack, which is what she did. I couldn't understand where she would sell my clothes.

"Kathy finally came home after four days and looked like shit. She was crying and real skinny and hadn't showered. She was sobbing as she told me how she had been good for so long, but the pressure had just got to her. I wanted to say, 'What pressure? The pressure of me baby-sitting your kid all goddamn day? The pressure of me paying your rent? What the fuck are you talking about?'

"But I knew. I knew what she was talking about. Sometimes the pressure is just inside of you and it grows and you don't know why; you can't see where it's coming from, all you know is that an explosion is approaching, and so you run. Kathy was like me in this way, and it scared me. I never got real mad at her—I couldn't. Fortunately for her, the rent was paid and the house was clean, so she could just crash.

"Two nights later I was at the Pool Cue Club with my friend Cynthia, who I met at the youth drop-in center. These two guys came up to us and seemed real nice. Their names were Buck and Milo. Buck was cute with a strong black ass and great eyes. They both wore tons of gold jewelry; rings, chains, earrings. They bought us drinks and paid for our pool. We let them drive us home. After they dropped Cynthia off at her grandmother's house, we were sitting in the car when Buck says, 'Do you want to go to New York?' It sounded fun and I really liked these guys, so I said 'Sure, when?' Milo said, 'Now.' An hour later we were in a suburb picking up Stacy, some other girl who was running away, and we were off driving to New York.

"Stacy was fifteen, loud, and dumb. I didn't really talk to her. Kathy had always told me how girls were brought to New York and turned into prostitutes, and for an instant I considered the possibility that Buck and Milo were doing just that to us. But they were too young, too nice, and had agreed to have me home by Wednesday, so I didn't think it could be possible.

"My crush on Buck worsened during the twenty-six hour car ride, and once when Stacy and Milo were sleeping he kissed me and put his hand up my sweater. Milo and Buck took turns buying what we needed. They bought gas, food, and cigarettes, and they even paid for hotels and big meals.

"When we got to New York we stayed at this big rundown hotel where some people lived full-time. Milo introduced me to Kristen, and when she started talking I knew we'd been brought there to be prostitutes. Kristen told me how for just one hour of work I could make three hundred dollars and have these fabulous clothes. We went through her closet, and her clothes were beautiful. They weren't all sleazy, either. She had some nice gowns, a mink stole, great silk blouses that cost at least one hundred dollars each, and probably twenty-five pairs of shoes.

"I knew what was happening, and I kept reminding myself that they just make it sound all glamorous, but it really is dangerous and sleazy. Still, somehow with Kristen and Linda, the other girl we met, it started to seem like it would be fun. They talked about parties they would go to with their clients and famous people they had met. Linda said she went on a date with Bonjovi. Kristen had seen Richard Gere and Patrick Swayze. It was all pretty amazing.

"I decided I needed to call Kathy for a reality check. I called her collect.

"'Kathy! Hi, girl—you'll never guess where I am.'"

"'New York,' she said.

"'How the fuck did you know?'

"'Look, girl, you are in some deep shit. Everyone knows Milo and Buck. You know what they're doing, don't you?'

"'It's not like that, Kathy. Milo and Buck are totally cool; we'll be back next Wednesday.'

"'*They'll* be back next Wednesday, without you.'

"'I'm not going to work like these girls out here. But Kathy, these bitches can make three hundred dollars an hour, and you should see their clothes.'

"'Child, I can make two hundred dollars an hour out of my apartment, and I have.'

"'I thought you quit that.'

"'Mostly... Honey, they're going to leave you out there. That's what they do. And after a few days you will be so helpless you will work for them, or their brothers, or their uncles, or whoever else knows who you are. Because you'll have nowhere to go and no one to save you.

"'Ask those girls how much of the three hundred dollars they get to keep. The answer is none of it, Michelle, *none*. I've seen this before. You didn't know Lori, but she's out there somewhere if she isn't dead yet. I went to school with her.

"'Probably some of those girls have AIDS. No, they probably *all* do.

New Yorkers fuck everything, and that AIDS bug is everywhere. Remember the movie *Paris is Burning?* Remember that girl who was into that glamorous life, prostitution and all, and they found her body three days after she had been strangled in some trashy New York hotel room? That movie was a documentary, Michelle. Documentaries are true. Don't think it can't happen to you.'

"Kathy knows just what to say to scare the shit out of me. I said, 'I know, Kathy— you're right—I know all that stuff is true. I'm coming home—don't worry, but it just doesn't seem that bad. In fact, it sounds pretty exciting when these girls talk about it.'

"'Yeah, well ask them how exciting the work is. You want some fat ugly man to stick his thing up you while you try not to puke or cry? Real exciting, Michelle. Welcome to New York.'

"I was scared, and trying not to cry. 'Well, what if they won't bring me home?'

"'Make up a story so they get scared they'll get in trouble if you don't get home. Tell them the cops are knocking at my door looking for you, you know, something like that. If nothing works, go to the police. They'll send you home.'

"Now I was thinking of what I might have to do to get out of there. But at the same time, I couldn't believe Milo and Buck were really pimp suppliers. Maybe they would just agree to take me home if I asked. 'Thanks, Kathy,' I said. 'I've got to go—we're going out. I'll be home soon, I promise. I'm glad I called. I love you.'

"'I love you too. Don't fuck around with this. Get home.'

"'I'll be home soon. 'Bye, Kathy.'

"At first I felt real awkward when I went back to the room. I was sure Milo and Buck could tell I was freaked. 'Where you been, Michelle?' Buck asked.

"'I went for a walk to buy some gum and cigarettes,' I said.

"'Don't go walking off without us, Michelle—this town is dangerous.'

"'I know,' I said.

"That night was great fun. I forgot about leaving and we just partied all night. Milo knew this limousine driver, and we did the whole town. We dropped Stacy off with some man she met through Kristen. But after we got back to the hotel I got nervous again. I told Buck that I needed to get home soon. I said there were warrants out for my arrest as a runaway, and that the cops had found where I had been living and had been asking my roommate where I was.

"Buck tried to convince me that I should stay in New York to hide. I said that Kathy had told the cops that I was out here with them, and that the cops had said that they could be arrested for contributing to the delinquency of a minor unless they got me back fast. Buck was pissed.

"'Goddamn it, Michelle, we can't just get up and leave in the middle of our vacation. We came out here for you, so you could have a good time, and now you want to mess it all up. Fuck, no.' I slumped against the wall and cried.

"In the middle of the night I heard Buck whispering to Milo and saying that they should leave right now. I froze in my bed. Those jerks really were going to leave me to wake up alone in New York. I listened some more and it was clear they were getting ready to leave in an hour or so. When Milo was in the bathroom and Buck was out of the room I grabbed my shit and ran down to the van. I knew where the extra key was, and I got in the van and sat in the back. They couldn't leave without me."

Michelle got home, but she could have just as easily been beaten up and left in the hotel room, or anywhere else in New York. Stacy, the other girl who drove out to New York with Buck and Milo, never came back as far as Michelle knew.

Luckily for Michelle, she is in some respects a strong survivor—she had enough of a self-protective instinct to flee danger, although not a moment too soon.

There have been books written about the traffic of girls to big cities to become prostitutes. Michelle hadn't read any of them, but she had heard about the practice through friends. Yet in spite of her awareness of this, Michelle allowed herself to flirt with the possibility of being lured into the life, and it took a caring and trusted authority figure to convince her to protect herself. Without her friend Kathy's expression of concern and care, the ending to Michelle's story could have been entirely different.

Kathy is a good example of how someone who has been through the experiences of street life can support a homeless youth. Kathy knew about prostitution and knew enough about the community Michelle was a part of to get the facts and present them to her. Because of these factors, Michelle listened to her when she probably would not have listened to a parole officer or other authority figure.

The perpetrators of sexual exploitation in Michelle's story understood what would lead street girls to trust them, and they capitalized on this. Buck and Milo were only slightly older than Michelle, so she was inclined to trust them merely because of their age. Also, the appearance of their support was appealing to her, especially since it was presented to the girls in a nonauthoritarian and noninstitutional way. Buck and Milo took on the appearance of peers who were giving Michelle a free trip with all expenses paid.

The girls who were already prostitutes appealed to Michelle's desire for glamour, great clothes, and a fast life—this is often a street kid's definition of success. Their tightly controlled lives were hidden, and the reality that Michelle would be living in an environment that was completely authoritarian and would leave her without respect or power wasn't heard until she called Kathy. Kathy explained how Buck and Milo would leave Michelle helpless and how she would have to work for pimps to get any of her basic needs met. Upon hearing this, Michelle finally realized the danger she was in. Fortunately, she was able to escape.

In the stories of David, Michael, and Michelle, the sexual exploiters began relationships by caring for the basic needs of the youths without delay, and without imposing expectations. Jerry, the man who had picked up David, provided immediate shelter. The johns who picked up Michael provided warmth in their car or homes, followed by an immediate financial reward which would allow Michael to purchase what he needed to survive. Michelle's favor was won over by Buck and Milo when they appeared to provide friendship and a free trip with all expenses paid. All of these exploiters had an understanding of what the youths needed, and how to earn their trust.

In the following story we will see how youths can introduce each other to dangerous activities and pressure them to get involved. Unlike Kathy and Michelle, Raul and Tim led each other into increasingly dangerous hustles. What they have in common with Kathy and Michelle is that they were merely trying to survive.

RAUL

I met Raul as an adult, and when he heard I was writing this book on homeless youth, he volunteered to tell me about his experiences as a street kid in Los Angeles. Raul is now a fitness trainer and cosmetologist. But he knows he is one of the few lucky ones—he has survived to reach adulthood and learned to live on his own.

"It felt good to have Tim around, but that didn't help get money for food, hotels, or an apartment. I had met Tim in Miami, where all the Cuban queens had fled to in the late 1970s during Castro's last exodus. Here in Los Angeles at age eighteen, we were broke again, and I had no one taking care of me. But I didn't want one anymore. I had been there, done that; I was finished being the kept boy I had been in New York City. My pattern had been to stay with older men until they were tired of me and then I was out again, with nothing. I was going to have my own life and not rely on anyone, but I needed money. Not three weeks from now after I had gotten a job, worked for two weeks, and got my first paycheck. No, I needed money in the next few hours for soap, food, cigarettes, and a place to stay.

"Tim had hustled in New York and Miami, and already, three days after we pulled in, he was hustling in L.A. He had told me about how it works, and he figured out the L.A. scene in about twelve hours.

"'Santa Monica Boulevard, near La Cienga, is the busiest,' he said. We were walking down Santa Monica Boulevard, and he'd look into all the cars and smile at the men while he spoke to me. 'Look, Raul, we don't have any choice—we need money now,' he'd say as he smiled and worked the cars. I know he was mad that we used his trick money for everything. 'If we both worked,' he said, 'we could get our own place in two weeks.'

"I knew exactly what it would feel like. I would have to act all turned on while I was either bored, scared, or disgusted. I remembered it well from the sugar daddies I had in New York City. 'I'll do it if you come with me,' I proposed to Tim, knowing it wouldn't fly.

"'Oh, good idea Raul, what will I do? Watch him suck you off? Stand there with a towel? No, honey, you have to do it on your own. Tell him to bring you back here when you're done. I'll wait at the corner of La Cienga and Santa Monica for you when I'm finished.'

"A car slowed down and pulled over. Tim went to the passenger window, leaned his head into the car, and talked while I stood at his side by the rear door looking around. I couldn't hear anything but traffic. The car was a black Audi with a briefcase and suit jacket in the back seat.

"Tim stood up and faced me. 'He's cool,' he told me, 'and he said he likes 'my friend,' so get in and I'll wait for you here.' Tim opened the passenger door, put his hand on my ass, and pushed me into the car. I cooperated, not wanting to make a scene and not wanting Tim to get angry. Tim closed the door, and the car took off. I felt sick to my stomach.

"I looked at the man, a dark-haired, fat, rich-looking man who I guessed was about forty. He offered me a joint. 'What's up?' I said."

Tim and Raul hustled on and off for a few years, then went in different directions. Raul eventually quit doing drugs and hustling, and today is living with his partner in Los Angeles. Tim killed himself two years ago with a drug overdose.

"Tim would get really depressed," Raul told me. "In the early years he was optimistic and hopeful, always energetic and funny. But in his twenties he bounced from one lover to another and never learned to be on his own—he never really quit using drugs or hustling. And one day I got a call from his old lover, saying he had stolen his car, driven to a parking lot, and killed himself."

OBSTACLES

avid, the blond punk youth brought to my office by an older man who was kicking him out of his house, had been on the streets more or less since the age of eleven. By the age of nineteen, he had developed specific desires, which you may recall: *"I want to have my own stuff, my own key to my own apartment where I can go and crash whenever I want and be safe from getting beat or rolled. I want to get my G.E.D. and work so I can pay my own way. I want to find a girlfriend and settle down."*

The interesting thing about David's list of wants is that aside from his desire to escape the violence of street life, it could have been that of any young adult. Young people just starting out on an autonomous life want essentially the same things. Like David, they want safety, security, independence, the skills or education necessary to get a job, and a family. Eventually, most street kids articulate these desires. When they first arrive on the street, however, they may not.

Street kids start off wanting to get away from whatever or who-ever is threatening their safety, security, or independence. They may run from violence at home, or leave a program where they have no pri-vacy or independence. Initially, their desire is often to "just get away." But as they learn through experience after experience that no one will take care of them on their own terms, they begin to discern what will help them live on their own and to value those commodities. David had reached that point. He had learned to value safety, security, privacy, and independence—things that had been scarce in his life.

This is not to say that David could easily break away from his street hustles and work towards independent living; far from it. The ability to overcome obstacles to legal self-sufficiency is separate from an expressed desire for independence. The ties holding a street youth in his current situation may be strong: gang connections, chemical dependencies, other lifestyle issues. There may also be emotional or intellectual barriers: a poor perspective on the future, hopelessness, a habit of running. Each obstacle to independence has its own solution, but each additional obstacle complicates the total picture. In coming to grips with what he wanted, David had simply accomplished the first step. He had articulated and demonstrated the desire for the things necessary for independent living.

In this section we will examine the process youths go through when they try to escape homelessness and work towards self-sufficiency. We will identify the common barriers, explore how they act as barriers, and discuss how they can be assessed in youths. Special attention will be paid to gang involvement, chemical abuse, street families, and internal barriers such as low self-esteem, hopelessness, habitual fleeing, and self-destructive impulses.

Let us start with what is agreed upon. There is little debate that if street youth are to become self-sufficient, they must essentially break their dependence on street culture; it is dangerous, and potentially fatal.

There is also little debate that efforts to help street kids should lead them away from relying on government entitlement programs and towards legitimate employment. (David articulated this desire himself when he said, "I want to get my G.E.D. and work so I can pay my own way.") Youths want to find alternative survival means to dangerous, violent, and illegal street hustles, but this means first breaking away from the obligations and entrapments those survival hustles entail. Eventually, this means holding a job—a job that provides enough money to live on.

Finally, there is little debate that before youths can work on independence, basic safety and security are required. More specifically, street youth need a place to live and sleep without a constant threat of violence—a place which will be available for more than a few nights. Such a place provides a home base from which a youth can work towards independence. The nature of street survival forces street kids to live in a hypervigilant and exhausting state of awareness that interferes with any planning or action to advance one's status.

Youth programs, government and legal agencies, and most homeless youths themselves agree on the need for safe housing, legal employment, and a break away from street culture. However, there is little agreement on the process and details of meeting those needs. Street youths have their own concepts of housing, work, and self-sufficiency, those who provide services have others, and those who fund the services have still others. For instance, street youth have their own idea of acceptable shelter and safety—one which is usually fairly minimal and self-determined, while providers often argue for greater supervision, sometimes including locked facilities. Education, job security, cultural assimilation, and social obligations are also common bones of contention. There are wide differences of opinion on how homeless youths should reach self-sufficiency and how that self-sufficiency should take form.

These differing perspectives on self-sufficiency means and goals complicate efforts to assist homeless youth. Too many institutions work at cross purposes, and too many efforts result in stalemate. In the end, the losers, of course, are the youths, who wind up on the streets in increasing numbers. Why are there such contrasts in perspectives? What can be done to unite them?

The segments of our population least comfortable with street youth measure the success of any effort to help them by their transformation into citizens who blend into mainstream culture. They often not only want street youth to subscribe to their own beliefs, but also to disappear for the conversion (perhaps to a remote rural location or to the military) and reappear wearing acceptable costumes of the working world, maternity dresses, wedding rings, and the like. On the other side of the spectrum, social service workers on the front lines marvel if a street kid can achieve financial self-sufficiency by legal means. The youth worker quickly recognizes the nose rings, shaved heads and other confrontational dress as innocuous, and learns to focus on immediate concerns.

Naturally, everyone is vulnerable to the flattery of imitation, and the street kid who begins to conform to our values is the one we feel ourselves liking the most. Education-oriented persons love the idea of a street kid who eventually goes to college. Bankers smile at the thought of a street kid who learns to save and invest his/her money. While not necessarily harmful, this perspective can become a problem when it overshadows the individual youth's desires.

Of the two perspectives mentioned above, it is that of the street youth worker which is most supportive for homeless kids. The youth worker goes out to meet street kids where they are, starts by simply building a friendship, and learns that to be effectively received, support must be provided from the bottom up and not from the top down.

Homeless youth have their own plans and visions. The most effective way to help them is to respect their desires, listen to where they want to go, and help them get there. A youth who wants to make a living playing the drums should be assisted in doing so. Assistance for such a youth might include information about opportunities for percussionists and introductions to drummers who are making a living at their music. A supportive case worker would process the new knowledge with the youth and assist him with school applications, rehearsal space arrangements, or a reevaluation of goals should he request it.

A youth with orange hair, a pierced nose, and black leather clothing does not necessarily need to "clean up" before she is employable. Many retailers, coffee shops, and entertainment places which cater to a young clientele will gladly hire a youth who projects a nonconventional image. An effective youth worker would help her refine her job interests and connect with potential employers.

On the other hand, programs that project predetermined values onto youths, such as standardized benchmarks of success, are programs that will lose them. For instance, in order for youths to receive services, many programs require him to be in school and either be working or looking for work. While these are admirable goals, they can backfire if the youth has not embraced them. As youths discern that there is little room for their visions, they will check out of services and seek what they see as a more respectful environment. This should come as no surprise, since most of them have done it before when they left homes, foster care, or other institutions.

In reality, all youth-serving programs contain elements of many perspectives, and the relative power of each determines the form and content of the program. As an example, government funding for homeless youth programs is contingent upon program compliance with well defined goals outlined by the government itself. However, there is always room for individual programs to argue for various forms of client flexibility. On the other hand, programs that provide street outreach workers and drop-in centers, while emphasizing youth-determined case plans, would not continue to get the finances necessary to survive without demonstrating progress to their funders in moving youths towards agreed upon social objectives.

To get a handle on improving services to help homeless youth, an awareness of the variety of youth-serving philosophies and power dynamics must exist. Who holds the power to shape the programs—the youths (including the data on homeless youth), the funders, and/or the administrators? How does public opinion shape programs? How do programs serve the youths, or the funders? What is a reasonable balance between the two? When are program requirements necessary for financial survival, and when do they assist the youths? These issues are critical because they determine the success and failure of every program in a financial sense, in getting youths to participate, and ultimately in helping them get off the streets.

As anyone on the front lines knows, youths are perceptive regarding the motives of those that offer assistance. They talk a lot about what people who offer assistance really want from them. They are experts at discerning which adults have their interests in mind and which merely make that claim.

In talking with Michael, the youth we met earlier who had likely contracted HIV from hustling on the streets of Minneapolis, he spoke of his ambivalence about taking his AZT to combat the infection. He said, "My doctor just wants everyone to see that he can get street kids to take medication. He's got something to prove to someone, probably all his doctor friends, about how good a doctor he is."

"So you don't think he is prescribing the AZT because it will help you?" I asked.

"I think he thinks he is, but he never asks me if I really want to live, or what else is going on in my life. He just assumes 'yes, of course Michael wants to take this pill that makes him feel sick every four hours for the rest of his life.'"

Michelle, as you may remember, questioned her father's motive when, after leaving her at a center for runaway youth and refusing to participate in any family meetings, he returned on the final day of her stay to prevent her from being placed in an institutional home for children. "If he really loved me he would have been there for the sessions, so we could work out the problems," Michelle said. "The only thing that mattered to him was that I didn't get placed in an orphanage. He couldn't deal with the guilt that would bring."

Part of learning to listen to street youth is becoming aware of their understanding of how the world works. Specifically, it means listening to their understanding of how and why things are provided for them. These excerpts from Michelle's and Michael's stories illustrate their understanding of why a particular significant person would "help" them.

To homeless youth, the motives of parents and service providers are always under question. The past history of abuse and neglect that both Michael and Michelle share is common among youths who believe that no one would do something for them without getting something in return. Whether these beliefs stem directly from abuse is up for debate, and is actually somewhat peripheral. The important point is that these beliefs are present and must be kept in mind during each interaction between a service provider and a youth.

CHAPTER

1

STREET GANGS

treet gangs are both a tempting trap and a formidable obstacle for homeless youth. While they may provide for immediate needs, kids who get involved in gangs are liable to accrue criminal charges, physical injuries, and chemical dependencies. Gang members also typically get involved in various hustles which they may become dependent on. Data from the Minneapolis Police Department indicates that homeless youths are often the front line laborers for street gangs in that city, performing much of the drug hustling, prostitution, and theft (fifty percent of gang members are under age eighteen, and many of these have no fixed address). Each gang-related scar impairs the youth's mobility towards legal self-reliance.

The Minneapolis Police Department estimates that by age eighteen, ninety percent of gang members have been arrested for at least one felony, and seventy-five percent have been arrested for at least two. A criminal history, of course, critically jeopardizes any future legitimate employment or hopes of renting housing. And yet a criminal history is only one way that gang affiliation complicates any attempt to achieve independent living.

In general, gangs do not value individual autonomy—the gang

comes before individual rights. As a result, gangs consider the property of a member to be the property of the gang. When a kid with an apartment or a car affiliates with a gang, or should a gang member acquire an apartment or car, these properties are put at the disposal of the gang. One boy in the Youth Housing Project described to me how, even before he realized that his new friends were in a gang, they had "borrowed" his apartment keys and made multiple copies. Within days they were using his apartment when he wasn't home.

Another obstacle to self-sufficiency posed by a gang is that gang activities take place predominantly at night. The gang lifestyle interferes with daytime employment, school, or the pursuit of social services. Gang members who sleep all day will expect the new member to work and party with them all night.

But the most damaging aspect of gang association is the conflict around lifetime membership. Leaving a gang (known as "dropping the flag") is very difficult for an affiliated member (like Jason, whose story is detailed below), and nearly impossible for an initiated member. Gangs have harsh initiation rituals and strict codes of loyalty, and membership is considered permanent. Leaving a gang is at the least seen as disrespectful, and is often perceived as a break in security. It is usually a violation of the gang's code, and is punishable by severe injury or death.

In spite of this policy of lifetime membership, however, new gang members are always being recruited. This is because by the age of twenty, sixty percent of gang members are out of circulation—they are either dead or serving long-term prison sentences. Older gang members—the survivors—typically find that reentrance into mainstream society is impossible because their criminal records are so dark.

While we do not know how many of the hundreds of thousands of youths on the streets are in gangs, we can guess that the number is significant. The Crips, the Bloods, the Disciples and the Vice Lords are not only present in most major cities; they often govern street life. They use violence against those who get in their way and extract thousands of dollars a week in "street taxes" from individuals who deal or hustle on their turf. They have more manpower and weapons than the police forces in many cities they occupy.

Youth service organizations and governmental corrections programs frequently view gang members as unreformable. The reason is not that gang members don't desire independence and legal self-sufficiency;

it is that these organizations and programs know that breaking from a gang is difficult. Agencies experienced with gangs frequently hold to the adage, "Once in a gang, always in a gang." And knowing what we now do about the few examples of gang detachment, the assumption that escape is unlikely is often realistic.

When I asked gang experts at the Minneapolis Police Department if they knew of any kids who had successfully broken free from gangs, they told me they knew of only a few. I have met only one: Jason, a young adult who now holds a job working with homeless youth.

JASON

In many respects, Jason's sixteenth year was his worst. After two unsuccessful foster placements within the same school district, he was back living with his parents. He was still on probation after his second major arrest for auto theft and burglary. Then came his increasing involvement with the Disciples.

His parents had learned to cope with their son by distancing themselves from him—often literally. They would take trips without him, let him skip school, and minimize their contact with him. He was home alone quite often.

A neighbor who was a member of the police force was aware of his record, and kept a casual eye on the house. One afternoon when Jason's parents were gone, he noticed that Jason had many visitors, most of them young African American men wearing the Disciples' colors: blue and black.

A week later, Jason was brought in on charges of possession and sale of cocaine. He had been caught dealing. His neighbor stopped in at juvenile detention to see Jason. He let him know about what he had seen, and Jason, feeling exposed, began to confide in him. Over the next few weeks Jason told his story, providing evidence to bust the gang on a number of charges. At the same time, the police's gang experts were making plans to get him to safety.

This is how Jason described his growing involvement with the Disciples:

"At first I was just hanging around with them after school. It was fun because they had money and girls all the time. They showed me how to wear their colors. We would drive around in these serious cars and stop and jam with homeboys everywhere. I couldn't figure what they wanted with a white dude, but I didn't worry about it too much."

Jason's puzzlement over what the Disciples would want with a "white dude" is understandable—the Disciples are an almost exclusively black gang. However, in the Disciples—as in other minority street gangs—white boys are present, although they are often second class members. Still, they are important; they are used as covers or avenues to suburban money. White kids can provide access to white parties and white drug traffic.

"It was amazing how much money these brothers had. They would carry rolls of twenties and hundreds. They were always real secretive about where it came from, but it was no mystery to me. Eventually one guy told me if I wanted to work for him I could make some real money, too. I knew what he was talking about—clockin' (drug dealing) and theft—but the money he had was unbelievable. I thought if somehow I could do it and get away with it for just awhile, I would quit.

"I was scared at first. But eventually he gave me some works and I rolled (sold) them to friends over a one week period. I got to keep four hundred dollars cash for about one day's work. That was more than I could ever make at any punk job I could get around town.

"I had hung with them for nearly all winter, but then something really bad happened. It was at night, and we were driving around in my car. Devon told me to drive up to the front of a store and go real slow because he was lookin' for this chick. So I did, and I wasn't really looking. Everyone was hanging out the windows and barking at all the babes, like usual. Then I heard this shot, and the whole car jerked. Devon screamed, 'Get out of here!'

"There were people screaming near the front door of the place, and I saw a crowd around a woman who was lying on the ground. I didn't realize the shot came from our car, but I was completely freaked. I turned to see if Devon or someone else in the car had been shot, and then I saw the gun. It was on his lap, hidden by his jacket. And I knew: he had done a drive-by, and I was involved. So I drove fast, and I was shaking, and I wanted to say, 'What the fuck are you doing, you idiot?' But I didn't—I was too scared.

"I drove out of the lot. Frank said from the back seat, 'Drive to Mitch's, they're waiting for us,' and I thought, *waiting for us?* It sounded like this had all been planned. I was shaking and I felt sick, and I couldn't believe they used my car for a drive-by. I just kept thinking, *These guys are really fucked up and I need to get away from them.* Well, I found out at Mitch's that it had been planned for weeks.

"I found out some other things at Mitch's, too. The Kingman took me aside and he said, 'We need to stay tight. You need Disciple's honor. This can't go nowhere, or we is all fucked. Saying a word to anyone is breaking honor and will be punished.'

"I got what he meant. What I was freaking about was the car—it was my car. They might trace it to my family, and then what?"

After that incident Jason was far too involved with the Disciples to get out. He vowed loyalty to the gang, and they threatened to kill him if he left. When he was picked up for selling cocaine, an inspection of his house revealed a gun and more of the drug. At the age of sixteen, Jason was in deep.

Because he confessed and provided information on gang activities, because an officer took a special interest in him, because his father was a powerful lawyer, and possibly because he was Caucasian, government attorneys and law officers worked together to get him away from gang life. It was successfully argued that Jason was manipulated into committing his crimes, and he was granted full immunity from the charges against him. Fortunately for him, he had no outstanding warrants, and his contact with out of state gang members was minimal. But both Jason and the police's gang experts knew it would take more to get him away from gang life.

He was transported in the middle of the night to Minnesota, to live with a relative. An alibi was made up and circulated among the inmates in detention that Jason had been convicted and sent to a juvenile prison in Illinois. At the time this was written, Jason had not returned to the state where he committed his crimes, and had stayed clean.

Assisting a youth in disassociating from a gang is a complicated and risky task. Jason's story illustrates the extreme precautions and extensive cooperation necessary for a clean break. A simple change of neighborhood or school would not have been sufficient, and might have jeopardized Jason's life; he needed to go where he would not be recognized by any of the Disciples he knew, and he needed to go quietly.

The Disciples and other gangs are often able to alert members across state lines to a potential AWOL, and their extensive traffic between cities enhances surveillance efforts. Jason needed to get out without any notice, because even out of state, the Disciples could cause trouble if they were alerted.

The final problem in getting Jason out of gang life was his record. He needed to stay out of corrections facilities, where gang members are pervasive, and he had to be admitted to a new school. This was his only chance, and his immunity allowed for it, but without it the transition would have been impossible. And, of course, few organizations or institutions are prepared or equipped to cooperate in providing the services Jason received.

For some youths whose affiliation is light, a change of neighborhoods and a conscious attempt to not associate with gang members may be sufficient. However, such cases are rare, and hard to detect. Most youths who are involved with gangs will minimize their involvement when questioned, and most will not see the urgency for a break, especially if their contact is light.

In the Youth Housing Project, we see additional gang-related problems for kids trying to make it on their own. As soon as they acquire an apartment, they become very attractive to gangs who are always looking for new places to party and run their hustles. The transition is fast—the new friends bring alcohol, cocaine, marijuana, and other gifts, and before he knows it, the youth's apartment keys have been duplicated and drug dealing is going on.

Most vulnerable is the black male youth who is alone and has time to hang out at arcades, parks, or malls. Caucasian males are often left alone unless their assets are clearly available and attractive. Females are pressured selectively.

But beyond race and gender, disassociation with family and the availability of free time and assets are the factors which predict gang involvement. The youths in our program who start off right away by going to school and working generally do well, and to our knowledge, none have gotten involved in gang-related activities. Others who have become involved in gangs have earned evictions within a few weeks after first being suspected.

Given what has been discussed in this chapter, it is no surprise that involvement in gangs is best curbed by prevention. Homeless youth must have knowledge about the long-term dangers of gangs, gang tactics, and signs of gang membership and activity in order to successfully avoid them. Youth workers must also be knowledgeable in order to direct vulnerable youths away from potential gang involvement.

For those youths already involved, breaking gang connections can be risky and even life threatening. Youth programs interested in helping kids leave gangs should do so only with the assistance of police and other local gang experts.

CHAPTER

SUBSTANCE ABUSE

The interference of chemical abuse with a street youth's efforts to establish self-sufficiency is substantial. Kids who hope to begin new lives with new jobs, schools, routines, friends, and responsibilities severely compromise their chances of success by abusing chemicals. Unfortunately, while living on the street, drug use is omnipresent and abuse is common. A 1990 survey of 185 homeless and runaway youth-serving agencies which was conducted by the National Network of Runaway and Youth Services found substance abuse to be the leading health problem among the youths served. In the Wilder survey of homeless youth in Minneapolis/St. Paul, fifteen percent of the youths interviewed had been admitted to a detox center at least once, while ten percent admitted to having a drug or alcohol problem. In yet another study, eighty-seven percent of homeless youths reported having abused drugs at some point.

Drug use on the street takes different forms than the kinds of drug use seen in high school students. Both populations abuse alcohol and pot, but street youth often use more dangerous and addictive drugs, including crystal (methamphetamine) and cocaine (including its smokable form, crack). The frequency and severity of use seen on the streets with kids like Jeff (whose story appears below) also goes far beyond common high school use.

The good news about drug use among street youth is that it often happens over a relatively short period of time; however, the substance use is often abusive. In other words, the use is usually excessive and has negative consequences, but severe physical dependencies are unlikely, as they do not have time to develop. In fact, much of the drug use among homeless youth could be categorized as experimental.

Studies vary, but drug use has not been identified as a major cause of youth homelessness; the heavy drug abuse taking place on the streets often originates on the streets. The following story, written by Jeff, a former street kid whom I met as an adult, bears this out. In it he tells about his use of crystal, or methamphetamine.

JEFF

"My involvement with a group of people on Washington Street in San Diego was short-lived, but it was very indicative of the intensity and pace of my everyday life as a drug-abusing homeless youth.

"One of the most surefire ways of finding a place to stay and/or your drug of choice was to get on the phone lines. Like every other city I've been to, San Diego has a profusion of 'chat lines,' or 'party lines.' Each of these lines has a 976 pay per minute charge as well as two or three free lines to ensure that there is always somebody there for the benefit of the paying caller. The free lines were highly valued by those of us who were out in the street, because they were an unfailing resource for people who desperately wanted company, drugs, and/or a place to stay. At any time of day or night you could call the line from a pay phone and not only find someone to stay with, but more often than not someone who would arrange transportation to their place.

"By this method I met Matt. I had called the line three nights in a row from the homes of the people I had stayed with the previous night, and on the fourth night I found Matt, who was looking for people to party with. Since I had called the line in the wee hours of the morning, it was simply assumed that the 'party' would include drugs that kept you up all night. I had grown to be intuitive about such things, and my assumptions generally proved to be correct. The party which ensued lasted about two or three weeks, and even today, six years later, it's a grim memory.

"Matt lived in a two bedroom apartment with anywhere up to six people at a time. Every month at rent time somebody simply sold some crystal and handed cash to the landlord. The amount of drug traffic through that house was unbelievable, and for me the place was a jumble of faces that never seemed to end. We basically lived on drugs: they replaced food, sleep, and the desire to do anything unless crystal was involved.

"During the day the place was fairly normal to outside appearances. Of course, the sight of someone doing household chores was usually that of a drug-crazed person who might vacuum the same patch of floor for hours on end, not realizing the passage of time at all. The reality of the situation was that nothing was normal; we were all definitely on a fast track to the end.

"Matt made some money as a disc jockey in nightclubs. Chico, another permanent fixture, was a transvestite by night, and would work the park for crystal. I would just walk endlessly at night, tricking or running drugs to kill time. All of us would wander home at three or four in the morning, usually do a few lines together, and then just sit around the place in a manic daze. I remember my body being so drained at times that I couldn't move, but my heart and mind raced uncontrollably.

"There were always other people, of course, but the three of us seemed to be the most permanent residents. The others would come and go in their transient way, moving from one drug house to another. Some got killed, arrested, or just disappeared. But for the three of us, the apartment became a trap. In our mental and physical condition we were no longer fit to be in public, and since we were controlled by our addiction we were afraid to leave anyway. We were forced to just watch each other waste away.

"It was near the end of the three week period that things erupted.

"One morning, when we were all lying around in a wide awake yet comatose state that passed for sleep, plainclothes police came to the door to arrest Matt. He had stolen a sixty-year-old woman's purse and pushed her down in the street, and he had lost his wallet in the scuffle. Chico, who had completely lost his mind by this time, began to scream and cover his face in the corner. The sight of him lying there with his makeup from the night before streaking down his face and his eyes void of all comprehension, combined with the sound of his shrieking in my ears, inspired blind panic in me. The police were just standing there, probably stunned by the spectacle, so I ran out the back door and down the fire escape.

"I continued to run down Washington Street back alleys, and then blindly until I found myself in Balboa Park. It was in the park that I finally lay down in a patch surrounded by dense bushes to rest and collect my thoughts, and I remember being grateful that I had thought to grab the crystal on my way out. This all took place roughly a month before my seventeenth birthday, a year after I had first run away from home.

"After a day or two I went back to the house to get a few things. I learned that Matt had escaped arrest on some technicality, but Chico had disappeared and was suspected dead. About a month later I learned that Matt had been found dead on the beach from an overdose."

Jeff continued to survive on the streets until he enrolled in the Navy at age eighteen. After being honorably discharged at age twenty-one, he resumed his previous level of drug use activity and had recurring bouts of homelessness. His years after the Navy were characterized by multiple job losses, evictions, and moves to new cities. Then, at age twenty-three and at the threat of another eviction, he went through a twenty-one day inpatient program for chemical dependency. Since that time he has held a job, received multiple pay raises, and maintained a stable living situation.

Jeff required professional chemical dependency intervention before he was able to stabilize. Even after being in the Navy, his consistent substance abuse patterns continued to endanger his safety and health, and prevented him from achieving any type of stability.

With street youth in general, there are two schools of thought on drug use intervention. The first and more conservative approach is the "wait and see" method. The youth worker may address the pitfalls of drug use or may even discuss the youth's drug abuse, but professional intervention or treatment is reserved until the abuse appears to be a chronic problem. The second and more aggressive approach mandates that chemical issues be addressed at the onset of any program.

The rationale behind helping a kid to stabilize before addressing substance abuse is that the abuse may be situational. Youths who use alcohol or other drugs on the street may not when placed in a stabilized setting with low access to chemicals and fewer street culture pressures.

As the statistics indicate, the pressures to use alcohol and drugs on the street are high. With eighty-seven percent of street youth abusing drugs, sobriety and abstinence can alienate a homeless kid from critical social connections. In Jeff's case, for instance, he would not have been able to use Matt's house for shelter had he not been using.

The only means to sort out the situational components of drug using behavior is to stabilize the situation and monitor the drug use. In the Youth Housing Program we have seen youths whose drug abuse abated once their lives had been stabilized.

The more aggressive approach seeks to assess chemical use upon intake and intervene according to accepted substance abuse/chemical dependency protocol. For a youth with a history of abuse, such an approach may make acceptance into a program contingent upon successful completion of chemical dependency treatment. Or, the program may incorporate chemical dependency treatment into its plan for self-sufficiency.

The advantage of the aggressive approach is that youth who have successfully completed drug interventions will have a better chance at success in any program. The disadvantages involve practical considerations and unnecessary interfacing with professionals. If nearly all street youth are abusing drugs, many are likely to be assessed as needing chemical dependency treatment before or upon being admitted into a transitional living program. However, full inpatient chemical dependency treatment programs can easily run up to ten thousand dollars per person. Given the difficulty of finding financial resources, entitlement program coverage, or insurance coverage for this population, such an undertaking is often cost prohibitive.

Certainly the individual situation of the particular youth is the most important consideration in determining a course of abuse or dependency intervention. That is to say, someone with a history of prolonged heavy use and other symptoms of dependency should receive prompt intervention, while the youth with a history of occasional chemical abuse might effectively be guided to address other more pressing issues first, such as housing, food, and finances.

Regardless of the approach of any particular program, drug prevention information should be readily available to all youth. This includes information about local Alcoholics Anonymous or Narcotics

Anonymous groups. NA and AA chapters in most major cities include specialized groups for youth, gays and lesbians, and other specific populations. In addition, NA and AA groups provide a family of support to achieve sobriety, and this is an important resource for most homeless youths.

Any youth who admits or recognizes her dependency and is receptive to assistance should be helped immediately. Waiting lists for substance abuse programs are unrealistic, especially when it comes to street kids. The window of opportunity during which they are both willing and able to accept help is almost always a small one.

CHAPTER

INTERNAL AND EXTERNAL BARRIERS

INTERNAL BARRIERS

Internal barriers to self-sufficiency are those barriers that homeless youths carry within their heads. In general, they are self-destructive habits or maladaptive cognitive patterns that interfere with progress towards independence. We have already touched on a number of them, including low self-esteem, hopelessness, emotional ties to street families and to certain hustles, a poor perspective of the future, and depression. They can result in such behaviors as fleeing, the return to drug use, or other forms of self-destructive behaviors.

Internal barriers are often more insidious and confusing to youth service providers than the more visible ones, like substance abuse and gang involvement. Unfortunately, few homeless youths are without a multiplicity of these barriers. Typically, once a youth has been situated with a job, school, and support, internal barriers surface in a number of forms; in fact, the presence of quietness or stability often seems to precipitate their appearance. In reality, their origins are more complex, and they are understood best when viewed from those origins.

Some internal barriers, such as habitual running or fleeing, are nonadaptive coping or defense mechanisms. Habitual running may have been learned at an earlier age, when running away brought attention to a family issue or protection from violence. However, while fleeing can bring temporary emotional relief, it can also result in legal trouble, the obliteration of any progress made in the previous setting, and building feelings of failure. The best approach in helping homeless youths deal with this tendency is to help them see the origin of their fleeing behavior and to assist them in developing new alternative coping mechanisms.

Other internal barriers, such as hopelessness and low self-esteem, are often reactions to previous failures, rejections, or abuse. These barriers can permeate the emotional state of the youth and affect all areas of life. A dysfunctional home, sexual exploitation on the streets, and failed placements are only a few of the common causes of hopelessness and low self-esteem in homeless youth. These barriers interfere with attempts at self-sufficiency by undermining motivation and permitting self-destructive behaviors. While steady progress towards reaching self-sufficiency goals can counteract these feelings, cognitive therapy, either in a group or individual setting, may eventually be needed.

Another complicated barrier to movement towards self-sufficiency for street youths can be their dependence on the charity of street culture and their commitment to their street families. The poor are often the most charitable, even while this quality contributes to their own poverty, and this adage proves true for many homeless youths. Despite the common belief that juveniles are self-serving and not respectful of others, many street youths acquire a strong sense of service to and protection of their street families. At the Youth Housing Project, the most common reason for eviction has been the recurring housing by tenants of other homeless youths. Some were routinely housing six or seven others in their small efficiency apartments. "Creating your own emergency shelter" is how we refer to it. And while some of this hospitality comes from loneliness, much of it comes from a sense of obligation to other youths.

The issues can be simple. Survival on the street often depends on friends helping friends in the short run, and not weighing whether helping them will complicate upward mobility in the long run. Most street youths, when given housing, are indebted to many others who have shared with them in the past. And when the friends that helped them when they were homeless suddenly become homeless themselves, it seems wrong not to shelter them. The same symbiotic relationship applies to other resources, including food, money, and even drugs. The commitment homeless youths have to each other runs deep. Like gang members, street youths often protect each other much more than their natural families do.

Yet another internal obstacle to self-sufficiency is emotional dependency on certain hustles—most notably prostitution. For girls, the trap of prostitution can be complicated, and can include a pimp or a gang. Prostitution for a gang provides a major source of gang revenue, and a girl involved in prostitution carries the same status as a secondary gang member. Accompanying this status, of course, are the same threats against leaving the gang. For most intents and purposes, girls who have prostituted in a gang setting should be considered gang members.

For boys, involvement in prostitution is rarely organized or enforced by a pimp, and the difficulty they have in leaving it is sometimes more an emotional than a financial one. Male prostitution is not known to be associated with gang activity; among homeless youth, male prostitutes often are self-employed hustling gay boys. It is the impression of many youth service workers that straight boys who are involved in prostitution do not have the emotional bond to prostitution that gay boys have. Even after the financial need is gone, many gay boys find it difficult to leave prostitution. Unfortunately, there is not enough information available to theorize why this is. By any standard, the situation is poorly understood.

For most homeless youths, a poor perspective of the future, or the inability to realistically visualize and plan one's future, is the result of a lack of a skill which comes with practice. Planning a future is both a tool and a luxury of those who have their basic safety and life-sustaining needs met. Many homeless youths, on the other hand, have lived in chaos, on the streets or at home, and as a result have never developed good future-planning skills. These skills are best taught gradually, through written and illustrated plans and timelines done by the youths. Positive accomplishments reinforce the value of future planning.

There are other internal barriers that are also skill-oriented.

They include poor decision-making skills, poor self-nurturing skills, and a lack of ability to exert a steady effort in a job or in school. Sometimes these barriers reflect underlying depression or hopelessness, but they often simply reflect a deficiency in basic skills. If not resolved with the onset of stability, underlying depression should be addressed professionally. Adequate skills, however, must be taught by an effective case manager or youth worker or, ideally, by other youths.

EXTERNAL BARRIERS

External barriers to self-sufficiency, including the lack of affordable or accessible housing, unemployment or underemployment, low wages, and the lack of educational opportunities, are barriers which are presented by our society. At least to some extent, all of them are imposed on homeless youth; the reality of those barriers to self-sufficiency is apparent to any family whose well-educated children keep coming home to live or need continued financial support.

Inasmuch as the barriers come from society at large, so must the solutions. Youth programs generally do not have the resources or power to address them. As advocates of youth, our responsibility lies in documenting and presenting the realities of these barriers to those with the power to make helpful changes: public housing authorities, school boards, government agencies, and lawmakers.

However, since the barriers also vary with the individual, they can be at least partially addressed on an individual basis. For instance, a homeless youth who has not finished high school can be encouraged and supported in pursuing education. Specific skill building help should be the focus of assistance programs, and those programs should reach out to youth who are ready to address the barriers keeping them from self-sufficiency.

Still, this approach does not deal with the problems inherent in our social welfare system when it comes to homeless youth. We will now proceed to explore a few of them, so we might better understand how policies need to be reshaped and redirected.

Entitlement programs such as General Assistance, Assistance For Dependent Children, Supplemental Security Income, Medical Assistance, and Section Eight housing are all designed in theory to assist persons whose incomes cannot cover basic needs. But when homeless youths are involved, such programs more often than not work as barriers to self-sufficiency rather than provide assistance. As a result, these programs are viewed by many youth workers as a double-edged sword.

Berhane's story of trying to access General Assistance in Minneapolis (detailed below) illustrates how these programs are often not prepared to assist persons under age eighteen. Their application processes can be difficult and humiliating. In addition, their benefits are inconsistent, require monthly paperwork, and are often reduced without notice. The self-sufficiency of most homeless youths is more often complicated by such programs than supported by them.

Fearing that entitlement programs breed system dependency, most independent living programs avoid government entitlements and work under the assumption that youth have the capacity to achieve self-sufficiency without such assistance. In fact, federally funded independent and transitional living programs are often prohibited from assisting youths who are receiving entitlements. For homeless youths with a low or nonexistent income potential, such as teenage mothers without partners and kids with significant health or educational needs, entitlement programs can be essential. These youths most often must rely on some governmental subsidy to make any progress towards self-sufficiency, and yet that very subsidy can block them from participating in independent living programs.

BERHANE

We first met Berhane, a seventeen-year-old legal alien from Ethopia, when we discussed youth homelessness resulting from poverty. After it became clear that he was entitled to housing through the Youth Housing Project, he and I began to investigate the possibilities of General Assistance and temporary shelter. He needed temporary assistance while he improved his English skills—his lack of fluency had prevented him from finding employment. I was also hopeful he would eventually qualify for subsidized housing, but he needed help in the meantime.

We had three tasks to accomplish that day I found him asleep in our office lobby. The first was to verify his lack of income from the AFDC office where his brother had collected on him as a dependent. Kiflu, his brother, had been collecting the assistance for the last three months, but had not supported Berhane. Verification would mean that Kiflu would lose the AFDC support, but Berhane did not care—he was mad at his brother for keeping the money. Besides, we were verifying the lack of support to qualify Berhane for the subsidized housing where he wanted to live.

The second task was to find him emergency shelter for the next few nights, and the third was to apply for General Assistance, which he would need for basic living expenses until he could work. Usually, in helping youths apply for entitlements, I let them tackle the system alone; I accompany them only if they encounter barriers. However, Berhane spoke poor English, so after letting him try to communicate his situation to the entitlement offices without success, I took the lead.

None of the tasks appeared to be difficult, yet all three turned out to be torturous.

At General Assistance we learned that despite the three week processing time, we could not submit his application until after his eighteenth birthday, which was in ten days. When I explained that he needed to be on some sort of assistance until then to qualify for housing, the desk worker said, "There is no General Assistance for individuals under age eighteen."

I knew this to be untrue. "Look," I said, "I know there's a juvenile GA program."

She was unimpressed. "Yeah, you can apply through family services, but they'll reject him because he's almost eighteen. Besides, he'd have to work with them on a case plan, which would take a while, and by that time he would be eighteen."

"Let me get this straight," I said as I formulated her information into an example that would clarify the irony. "Since Berhane is almost eighteen, no one working with juveniles will help him, because by the time the help goes into effect, he will be too old. But in the meantime, the adult divisions won't work with him or even begin to process his application because he *isn't* eighteen."

"That's right," was all she said.

"Doesn't it seem that the logical thing would be to start processing the application for adult benefits now, so that he won't have to wait for weeks after he turns eighteen before he can get money to live?"

She stared at me blankly, noticeably bored by my critique of the welfare system. "Look, sir," she said in an annoyed voice, "these are the rules. I can send you to family services if you like, but it won't do any good."

I sensed defeat, but I asked anyway: "Can we at least get him vouchered for some shelter in the meantime?"

"Unaccompanied youth are not allowed in shelters."

I pretended to be stunned by the news, but I had actually expected it. "Oh, how humane," I said.

Then she offered us some helpful, if contradictory, information. "There is one shelter that can house some youths, but this office isn't authorized to voucher youth into it. Have you asked his AFDC worker?"

"No," I said, "but I guess we should." We left.

At the AFDC office, eight blocks from the General Assistance office, I asked again. "How can I get an unaccompanied seventeen-year-old vouchered for emergency shelter until I can get him into permanent housing?"

The receptionist told me, "We don't voucher unaccompanied youth into shelter here." Once she had said this she appeared to be done providing information.

"Any suggestions?" I prompted.

"Well, you could talk with his case worker, but I know we don't voucher unaccompanied youth. Who is his case worker?"

I looked to Berhane. "A man with an American name—I do not know," he said.

I felt stupid now, because I had this man's name on Berhane's paperwork back at my office. "Something Collins?" I guessed.

She said directly to Berhane, "If you don't know your caseworker's name, use the phone in the hallway and call the number under the sign that reads, 'Worker Unknown Number.'"

We schlepped to the hallway, both feeling foolish for not knowing the caseworker's name. Not surprisingly, the hallway was crowded with people waiting in line to use the one phone.

Just beyond the phone was the door behind which the caseworkers all appeared to live. The lettering on the door read, EMPLOYEES ONLY—ALL OTHERS MUST BE ACCOMPANIED BY A CASEWORKER. As I waited in line I pondered the phrase, "must be accompanied by a caseworker." In all other circumstances I could think of, the phrase "must be accompanied by" was followed by the words, "parent or guardian." Why had they chosen this phrasing for the message on the door? I was convinced that the implication was that your caseworker was your parent or guardian—not your advocate, not your partner, but your superior.

As we waited in line, we saw an occasional caseworker slip in and out of the door. The fear that they would be recognized by one of their clients in the hallway was quite evident on their faces.

After a forty-five minute wait in line, I was still not prepared for the busy signal I heard after dialing the "worker unknown" number. Trying to contain my frustration, I slowly walked to the end of the line. When was the last time I had heard a busy signal? In this era of call waiting, call holding, and automated messages with touch tone access, a busy signal seemed archaic, unnecessary, and under the circumstances, rude. This inconvenience seemed very unnecessary, and felt intentional. All in all, General Assistance was rating very low on any scale of customer service quality.

I did not want to wait in line again, and I considered driving back to my office to get the caseworker's name. First, though, I decided to approach the counter again. "What is the alternative to the 'unknown caseworker' number?" The receptionist looked perplexed. "The line is busy," I explained.

"The alternative is to try again."

Berhane stepped in. "Can't you just look my name up on the computer in front of you?"

She did not say "no." Instead she said, "It is your responsibility to know your caseworker's name. You have to have *some* responsibility." As if the lives of all AFDC recipients were void of responsibility—or worse, that all recipients were completely irresponsible, and it was the job of AFDC to *teach* responsibility. I could see this attempt at humiliation for what it was, but I doubted whether Berhane was quite so immune to it.

Two hours later, we finally did get verification from Berhane's caseworker that his income level was zero. The caseworker was cooperative, but this verification committed neither him nor AFDC to anything. He referred us to Child Protection for emergency shelter vouchers.

Back at the Youth Housing office we called Child Protection Services. One hour later, an intake worker called us back and referred us to Family Services. A second hour after that, an intake worker from Family Services returned our call. She asked, "What happened? Did he run away from home?"

"Not exactly," I replied.

She said, "Well, here at family services we would have to work with the family and try to figure out how we could get them back together. Where is his family?"

"Most are in Ethiopia," I said.

"Well, why did he leave who he was staying with?"

"Three persons—two married adults and a seventeen-year-old boy—were living in an efficiency apartment. I'd say the problem was related to poverty."

"We aren't equipped to deal with that. He would have to go through Project OffStreets. They could voucher him there."

"My client is resistant to going there for cultural reasons." Berhane knew none of his Ethiopian friends were at Project OffStreets, and he felt uncomfortable. "Are there alternatives?"

"No."

Berhane continued to sleep outside.

This story raises many issues about entitlement programs. I will let it speak for itself about the inappropriate and patronizing attitudes of many of the workers we encountered. What struck me more was that there was no sense of responsibility to the hungry or homeless. The response to pleas of desperation was, "That's how the rules are." The programs were all being run from an exclusionary perspective; the workers appeared to focus on excluding people rather than on including them.

The attitudes of the workers was not the only humiliating aspect of the experience. The lack of knowledge they exhibited of other programs was disrespectful of the applicant's needs and time. The ultimate negative answer that should have taken minutes took hours because of false leads and misinformation.

Despite the fiasco just described, I will not hesitate to mention that for those who can bear the frustration, entitlement programs do offer some sustaining services. Berhane did eventually get approved for subsidized housing. He was then able to attend English as a Second Language classes with others from Ethiopia. Within a few months after that, he found work.

This book is an attempt to sort out the issue of homeless youth. There are few known answers. Assisting youth in the transition from homelessness to self-sufficiency is a challenging task with few proven methods. In order to be effective, services must provide everything a stable family provides, while also providing crisis intervention and a familiarity with the realities of street life.

This agenda is quickly evaluated as insurmountable by many programs and agencies. Adding to the complexity of the transition necessary to meet the needs of homeless youth is the rudimentary state of the knowledge base on street life and street kids. Programs focused on independent or transitional living situations for youth are few, and those that do exist are brand new. Even in the largest cities where the problem of homelessness among youth is epidemic, these programs have been around for only a few years.

In the next section we will take a deeper look at some of our societal responses to the crisis of homeless youth. We will look at programs that challenge the capabilities of the system, and at various efforts to create housing for youth. Finally, we will examine the newest efforts, the transitional living programs for homeless youth that are just now capturing the attention of the youth service community and are beginning to command both attention and funding.

RESPONSES

According to most states' laws, parents are to provide basic needs, including food, shelter and clothing, for their children until age eighteen (and under some circumstances longer). Also according to most states' laws, government becomes responsible for children when a family is unable to care for them, although only after formal legal proceedings that vary from state to state. Unfortunately, the reality is that there are many youth who are not being provided basic necessities by either family or government.

In government agencies, older kids often fall through the cracks. An administrator of a county funded emergency shelter service for children in Minneapolis put it the following way:

"Ten years ago the county didn't give up on older kids, age fifteen or sixteen—now they do. When they run, they're gone, and no one keeps track anymore."

This reality was also reflected by his counterparts who are employed by the county: "Hennepin County will not chase an older kid to provide him with housing or services, but if he calls, we will assist him," said one county worker. "By age fifteen, many youths who have been in the system are out; they have run and we have lost track of them. The numbers of older youths, as well as the costs and obstacles to assisting them, have become overwhelming. Besides, many youths have been through what we have to offer and they are not interested."

Looking at the cost of current services, it is easy to see how governmental care for children could overwhelm any state budget. In Minnesota alone, the institutional care of children represents a one hundred million dollar cost to taxpayers. State wide, more than fifteen thousand kids are cared for, eight thousand of those in foster care.

In Hennepin County, which includes Minneapolis and much of the surrounding metro area, foster care families receive between $425 and $1,100 per month per child (the rate increases with the age of the child and difficulty of care). The cost of group homes averages between $70 to $90 per day, or $2,100 to $2,800 per month per child. Residential treatment centers receive between $100 and $125 per day, or between $3,000 and $3,750 per month on average. Some programs receive higher compensation because of larger staff and greater treatment and supervision capabilities. Adolescents, largely because they are more likely to receive a group home or facility placement, are the most expensive children to house, and they often run away from all three types of care, including foster homes.

In comparison, transitional living programs (TLPs), the newest form of housing services for youth, are much less expensive than foster care, group homes, or residential treatment centers. They are also the youths' preferred form of housing assistance. Transitional living programs set up an older youth in an apartment and assist her with school, work, and independent living skills. Some programs use scattered apartments sites and migrating supervision, while others congregate youths in a building and provide on site supervision. Regardless of which form is used, TLPs are designed to assist youth in the transition from homelessness to independent living.

The direct cost of transitional living programs for youth are often little more than the cost of the apartments. Transitional programs provide one youth social worker for ten to twenty youth at a fraction of the cost of the one worker to three to six youth ratio seen in group homes or institutionalized care. The administrative costs of transitional living programs, because of the relatively small front line staff, are also much less than for other types of care.

In the first year of the Youth Housing Project, the transitional living program for youth started at Central Community Housing Trust of Minneapolis, we provided a complete program with a part-time case manager for up to five youths at a time at a cost of $10,000 per year. We provided assistance with housing, school, work, and accessing support and health services for an average of three months per youth, and the average cost per youth per month was $333. This cost is significantly lower than the $425 to $1,100 per month for foster care, or the minimum $2,100 per month for group homes or $3,000 per month for residential treatment centers.

Of course, the youths that succeed in transitional living programs are those who are motivated and have the capacity to live independently. But from what we know about them, homeless kids are already highly skilled at living independently—albeit not legally or safely. Transitional living programs work with their desire to live independently and help them by making living easier, safer, and more autonomous; we have found that a large percentage of older street youths who come to our door wanting to be part of the Youth Housing Project are quite willing and able to do what it takes to live independently.

Later we will discuss transitional living programs in greater depth, and explore how they differ from the more common approaches which prevail today. First, however, we need to examine the programs and facilities which have historically been our responses to disenfranchised youth. Their pitfalls reflect how society has perceived homeless kids, and their failures can serve to show how our responses need to be modified.

CHAPTER

THE CURRENT SYSTEM

efore they are homeless, most youths spend time in out of home placements. In the Minnesota Wilder study of homeless youth, 60% of the youths surveyed reported that they had previously lived in one or more out of home placements. The most common placements were foster homes (38.3%), followed by detention/correction facilities (31%), residential treatment facilities (22%), mental health hospitals (18.5%), chemical dependency treatment facilities (14.8%), and halfway houses (10%). Data from other populations of homeless youth around the country show similarly high rates of previous out of home placements. Whether the nature of these out of home placements *causes* homelessness is unclear. However, the high percentage of homeless youths who have been in placements does suggest some connection.

Before we can begin to speculate how out of home placements affect youth homelessness, we must first explore how youths are placed there, what their typical experiences are, and how and why they leave.

ADMISSIONS

There are three general types of care facilities which teens find themselves channeled into as they separate from their families: mental health facilities, correctional facilities, and general care facilities (foster care or group homes). However, the distinctions between types can be fuzzy. Each of them refer youths back and forth, often based on capacity and payment politics. Many youths have lived in more than one type of facility. Youths from more affluent families usually go to private facilities initially, while poor youths are placed in public service facilities right away.

The first stop for many youths in Minnesota's Hennepin County is St. Joseph's Home for Children. Many kids, from infants to age seventeen, are sheltered at St. Joseph's while arrangements are made for foster care or some other placement. St. Joseph's is a major avenue into the governmental child care system which houses more than fifteen thousand children in Minnesota, eight thousand of those in foster care.

While family reunification is the priority, St. Joseph's acknowledges that this often isn't realistic or safe; between thirty and fifty percent of admitted children have a history of being abused. Abuse, along with parental neglect and abandonment, are the primary reasons for admission. Nineteen percent of the youths arrive without any permanent address, and those youths with histories of abuse or no permanent address are likely to receive out of home placements.

Still, access to St. Joseph's is limited. The facility does not accept walk-ins, and children must be referred through the police or a social worker. Similarly, the out of home placements that take youths from St. Joseph's also do not accept walk-ins. In fact, most out of home placements require a referral, and thus are not accessible to youths on their own. As a result, many unaccompanied teens in the Minneapolis/St. Paul area turn to youth emergency shelters, like the Bridge for Runaway Youth or the Lutheran Social Services Safe House. However, the total capacity of each of these accessible emergency youth shelters is approximately fifteen.

This is not to imply that street kids are banging on the door of St. Joseph's trying to get in. Most know that access requires a police officer or social worker, and this serves as a deterrent. Most are also aware that while the facilities are not locked, admission will mean that their lives will be regulated, they will receive counseling and testing, and they will run the risk of being placed in other, more restrictive settings.

For some youths who do not get the attention of a social worker or the police, placements are still possible. Admission to health care facilities, including hospitals and chemical dependency treatment programs, is often facilitated by parents and by the health care system itself. One example from my personal experience as a medical student on the wards of a local hospital's psychiatric unit supports this conclusion.

In 1989, as a fourth year medical student, I was assigned to admit a fifteen-year-old boy for depression and suicidal tendencies. His mother had contacted the hospital and said she had read his journals and was alarmed at the number of times death appeared in his writing. She was also concerned that his behavior was rebellious and reclusive.

Upon interviewing the boy, I noted a normal fifteen-year-old who denied drug use, current suicidal thoughts or feelings of depression. He spoke instead of conflicts with his parents over curfew and responsibilities, and described his mother as hysterical and overprotective. He said he had written the journal entries in question over a year before, when he was trying to write lyrics for his band.

While I believed he was minimalizing his thoughts about death, he did not appear to be depressed or suicidal. His psychiatric evaluation for depression revealed that he had only one of the nine listed symptoms—difficulty in falling asleep. According to the American Psychiatric Association, in order to be diagnosed as having major depression, he needed to display five of the nine symptoms over the past two weeks. However, after presenting my findings to the staff and recommending outpatient family therapy, I was told that he would be admitted and treated for depression based on his one symptom and his mother's assessment.

Anti-depressant medication was prescribed, and he was diagnosed as suffering from major depression. He was in the hospital for two weeks, and under the influence of antidepressants, he slept alot and became very compliant. He was then discharged back to his family, after his mother had calmed down significantly. The total hospital cost was likely between ten and twenty thousand dollars.

In this one example, questionable judgment was exercised a number of times, starting with his admission. The boy's opinions went unheard, his denial of depression and his confession of family problems unnoticed. Instead, his mother and a physician were allowed to remove him from his home and place him in the hospital. Upon admission, he was labeled with a serious mental disorder and medicated.

What this seemed to accomplish best was to satisfy his mother.

This boy's future interactions with the health care system may be tainted, and given his experience with it, the reaction will be justified. The lesson he may well have learned could be not to trust, but to resist. His mother, on the other hand, learned that she can put her children away by protesting strongly enough, and that they will not be listened to if they contradict her.

If family relations continued to deteriorate and the boy were to eventually become homeless, it could be argued that the health care system had played a part in the process. After a hospitalization such as this, a family may begin to feel a lesser responsibility to a child, leaving the impression that the problems are the child's alone—not the whole family's. This is a direct setup for premature family severance and resulting youth homelessness (as well as a gross waste of health care dollars).

The story just related is by no means unusual; many street kids have their own similar ones. Diagnoses and admissions for depression, bipolar disorder (manic-depression), and even schizophrenia are common. Less severe nonpsychotic diagnoses, such as conduct disorder, adjustment disorder, and nondependent abuse of alcohol or drugs, are even more widespread. Numerous studies from the 1980s document substance abuse admissions for adolescents given the diagnosis "nondependent abuse of alcohol or drugs." Given what we now know about chemical dependency, most of those hospital admissions are likely to have been unjustified. As insurance reimbursements have become more selective, the criteria for hospital admission have tightened, and a diagnosis which justifies a hospitalization must now be more severe. One consequence is that the resulting diagnostic labels are more debilitating.

Unjustified admissions and inappropriate placements are also common in both social services and corrections. John, a nineteen-year-old boy who was interviewed for the 1992 Hennepin County video, *Perspectives on Youth and Homelessness*, described his placements this way:

"I haven't been with my family since I was eight years old. I was an abused child, so I didn't work out too good in school or with other people. I was in a mental institution for four years, and that was kind of a crazy place. I was always running from there. They had me on the maximum security ward for three out of the four years, and I was still running. I found ways to get out.

"After that they put me in DYS—Division of Youth Services. That's a place for teenage criminals. But I wasn't no criminal—I never had no record until I turned eighteen. But nobody wanted me, so that's where they had to put me."

I had no way to check on the official reasons for his progressively more restrictive admissions, but if John had continued to "find ways to get out" as he said, he would have qualified as a "criminal" solely on the basis of his repeated running.

Kim, a seventeen-year-old African American girl who appeared on the same video, also talked about how her running away had been dealt with:

"I've been locked up alot of times—for running away, and I've been locked up for emotional problems, for being a manic-depressive. But mostly for running away. I don't think anybody should have to get locked up for running away. I mean, a lot of times I run away because of things that happen at home, but maybe it's the parents who should be locked up sometimes. It's never the victim's fault, but people don't really believe that. I do, because I've been a victim."

I've spent time with both John and Kim on a number of occasions. John impressed me as a conscientious boy who had learned how to survive independently by panhandling and selling junk. His personality was warm and engaging, and he shared many stories about how he had taken care of other youth and shared his resources. He was quite open about the crimes he had committed since age eighteen, talking freely about stealing, breaking and entering, and prostitution. Kim, while a little more distant, was clear and articulate about the injustices she had seen committed against herself and others. Her mood, thought pattern, and history gave no evidence of the mental disorders with which she had been diagnosed in earlier years. She did, however, show a great deal of her mistrust towards hospitals, correctional facilities, and other programs.

Looking back, both youths continued to feel that their placements had been unwarranted and abusive. They saw running away as the major transgression which had caused the bulk of their placements. As he indicated in the video, John also believed he had sometimes been placed in correctional facilities because there was nowhere else for him to go. Both explanations for placement are likely true.

There is mounting evidence that many placements are not just unpleasant for youths; they are abusive or otherwise inappropriate. Psychiatric and substance abuse programs have been under the greatest fire lately. One study in an 1989 issue of the *Journal of Adolescent Health Care* states, "There is mounting evidence that many of these inpatient placements are inappropriate, that large numbers of young people are being deprived of their liberty under the guise of receiving medical treatment without the benefit of due process or procedural safeguards, and that the quality of care in many hospitals is poor and abusive." The article explains that some hospitals, in order to combat falling admissions and profits, are resorting to unethical and unprofessional tactics to assure a "share in the market."

WHY YOUTH RUN AND DON'T COME BACK

When homeless youths who have run away from placement are asked why they ran, they articulate a number of reasons. In the case of foster homes, it is often because those with a history of abuse find them very uncomfortable. Youths who have been betrayed by past family members find it difficult to trust any parental figures or assimilate into any family unit. Group homes are often run from because the youths feel trapped and overregulated (group homes are usually not long-term arrangements and do not foster long-term supportive parental relationships for youth). More institutional care, such as regional treatment centers or correctional facilities, are described by some youths as prisons where there is no privacy. Days are tightly scheduled, therapy regimens are mandatory, and shared sleeping and dining facilities are the norm. Youths often feel as if they are being treated like criminals for no reason. Hospitals for mental health and chemical dependency issues are run away from for similar reasons.

Once they are out on their own, older homeless kids rarely, if ever, contact the county. County workers explain this in one way—kids explain it in another.

One county worker told me about Susan, a 16-year-old girl who had been in the foster care system for five years. "She ran, and no one heard from her for six months. By the time her foster family got word from her, she was very streetwise and was entangled in the 'glamour' of street life. She had been raped and assaulted, but she wanted the fast life, with the cash and the drugs. What Hennepin County has to offer will never be as exciting."

As you might guess from the stories of street kids in this book, homeless youths explain their reluctance to return to county services somewhat differently. They describe how contacting the county may result in an unwanted placement—most likely in an arrangement they had run from before. Reconnecting with the county could also result in an arrest or detainment for any number of minor law violations that most street kids accumulate, including running away. Finally, reconnecting might result in another misguided mental health or chemical dependency hospitalization, and it will almost certainly mean a loss of privacy and independence and the beginning of authoritarian rules and regulations.

DISCHARGE FROM OUT OF HOME PLACEMENTS

For those who do not run from out of home placements, discharge is often equally traumatic.

At St. Joseph's Home for Children, discharge comes the day of a youth's eighteenth birthday. Some have been in the care of the county for years, and are not in contact with any family members. Most, being legal adults, are not discharged directly to families, and unless further treatment is necessary, they leave to live on their own. Unfortunately, many do not have the skills or education to survive independently by legal means. There are few services from the county home to assist these youth with independence, and what services do exist are poorly funded. So, as in many other states, they become the new homeless.

The workers at St. Joseph's pool their resources and often donate some basic furnishings and supplies to youths upon discharge. One worker described to me how someone on staff takes charge and collects pans, utensils, other kitchen supplies, bedding, and basic furniture so it can be presented to the youth at the eighteenth birthday party. "We know they need more," he said. "They need an apartment, a job, some savings, and a belief in themselves that most of them do not have. It seems kind of hopeless, but the rules are 'out at eighteen.'"

The efforts made by the workers at St. Joseph's Home for Children obviously go beyond what their jobs require. The fact that they exceed what is normally done to help young adults live independently is a sad statement on the current system.

Often with the best intentions, we have created institutions and programs which not only fail to adequately address the needs of homeless youths, but often let them fall through large holes in what is supposed to be society's safety net for the disadvantaged. In the next chapter we will look at what can be done to transform what can only be described as an inefficient, costly, and largely ineffective social welfare system for youth.

CHAPTER

WHAT NEEDS TO BE DONE

In the last few years, eight million dollars annually has been made available by the U.S. Department of Health and Human Services through the Administration for Children, Youth, and Families, and through runaway and homeless youth programs. A portion of this money is allocated for transitional living programs for homeless youth throughout the country; some of it goes directly to specific programs, while some is awarded to governmental entities for distribution.

Two transitional living programs in Minnesota have received such funds, and together have been able to provide assistance for close to one hundred homeless youths each year in the Minneapolis area. Unfortunately, the best estimates of the number of homeless kids in the area is between fifteen hundred and two thousand on any given day, and many youths who want the kind of assistance these programs provide are turned away daily. A portion of the one hundred million dollars spent in Minnesota alone for the institutional care of children needs to be reallocated towards transitional living programs.

Unfortunately, counties and states are slow to support transitional living programs for youth, for a number of reasons. Most of them are political or based on outdated assumptions.

Transitional living programs challenge the basic premise that other county and state programs are based on: namely, that homeless youth are ill and need to be cured. Group homes, regional treatment centers, and other institutions are *treatment programs* that employ costly intervention techniques to address the pathologies of homeless youth: their impulsiveness, their need to challenge authority, their tendency to run, and others. Treatments also include therapies for a number of pathologies which may be falsely perceived by the mental health community. These include adjustment disorders, conduct disorders, depression, schizophrenia, bipolar disorders, and borderline, histrionic and antisocial personality disorders.

In contrast to most established youth facilities, transitional living programs work from an assumption of health. They maintain that many youths on the street are healthy, and that their primary need is housing. While many homeless youths exhibit "symptoms" of mental illness or maladjustment, many of these are situationally dependent—natural responses to life on the street or a history of abuse. Transitional living programs believe that these "symptoms" are often resolved when the youth is heard, given what he needs, and stabilized.

In the experience of the Youth Housing Project, this has regularly turned out to be the case. Many youth in our transitional living program thrive when given the freedom and support to make their own decisions and to control their own lives. Hopelessness and chaos is replaced by a sense of pride and self-sufficiency. Of course, many youths do not escape their pasts mentally unscarred. Even after prolonged success in a transitional living program, most continue to experience bouts of low self-esteem, depressed feelings, anxieties, and compulsiveness. But the approach of the transitional programs is not to make these "symptoms" the focus of the program, but instead to approach whatever issues remain after stabilization with balanced interventions. Often these interventions are suggested by the youths themselves.

When I am counseling a youth who is dealing with recurrent feelings of loneliness and isolation, for example, my question to him is, "What do you need?" If he does not immediately know, I ask directed questions to allow him to identify his needs. Questions like: "What thoughts are you having when you feel down?" and "What activities help you feel better?" We then try to address the unmet needs in a variety of ways. They may include broadening his social connections by introducing him to a support group for youth dealing with HIV infection, to a group for Adult Children of Alcoholics, or to some other peer support organization. If appropriate, we would discuss sliding scale mental health counseling, from psychiatric evaluation to therapy and temporary medication. The key difference between the transitional living approach and others is that it is more gradual, more youth-directed, and much less traumatic than being uprooted and placed in a group home or hospital.

Transitional living programs represent another basic difference in their approach to helping homeless youth. They recognize that a youth's most important need, once basic necessities are met, is a set of skills which will allow her to live as a self-sufficient adult. Other programs focus on treatment of the youth's problems and often neglect, in part or whole, how the youth will live when discharged.

In addition, programs which are attempting to address the need for independent living skills are finding resources hard to come by. At St. Joseph's Home for Children, Hennepin County's largest child shelter, efforts are made when a resident turns eighteen to assist him with independent living. As we've seen, workers at St. Joseph's take in-house collections to help youths acquire basic necessities, and while they have tried to create funded programs, their one existing effort, Operation Success, which assists youths ages ten to seventeen with job search and application skills, is dangerously underfunded and may go under.

For youths in foster care, there is no government support whatsoever for follow up or independent living services. Legal AIDS Society of Minnesota, a frequent advocate of homeless youth, has recognized this deficiency in services for years. Recently they facilitated the legislative passage of an addendum to foster care regulations requiring foster care to include a plan for independent living after discharge.

Part of the resistance to supporting transitional living programs for youth comes from political inertia. Foster care, group homes, treatment centers, corrections facilities, and hospitals all are established institutions with powerful lobbying forces. Their lobbying may be used to secure funding, but it also prevents the germination of new programs. As an example, St. Joseph's Home for Children has recognized for years that older youths need independent transitional housing, but when St. Joseph's made an attempt to address this need with its own plan, it was squelched by foster care advocates who compared the effort to the creation of orphanages.

Resistance to transitional housing programs for homeless youth can also run quite deep in neighborhood groups and business committees that base their opposition on negative expectations. In 1991, a vacant apartment building was donated for use by homeless youth to the Central Community Trust Youth Housing Project in Minneapolis. It needed extensive renovation, but presented a great opportunity to house twenty-eight youths. The building was ideal in its size, location, and design—and it was free. It was near the downtown area, and would provide good access to youth services, employment agencies, jobs, alternative schools, and the YMCA. The neighborhood was by no means exclusively residential, so I did not expect a great deal of resistance. I was wrong.

At a meeting where I presented the plan for the Youth Housing Project's building renovation to the neighborhood business organization, I was listened to politely and then voted down nearly unanimously. In their denial of support, even though they had no professional assessments on the condition of the building, they contested that the building was too deteriorated for renovation. The Youth Housing Project, on the other hand, had building engineers' assessments which indicated that renovation was a reasonable goal.

I had wrongly anticipated that the most likely areas of resistance would be neighborhood security and parking, so my co-workers and I had done special work on these two issues. We had planned a tight security system, including a twenty-four hour on-site security person. We offered to work with the neighborhood to raze the empty commercial building directly across the street, which would provide many more parking spaces than the apartment building's lot alone. But despite our preparation, another reason was found to oppose the project. In retrospect, I can only wonder whether their resistance was really caused by fear of the youths.

So today, in Minneapolis, we have a seventeen car parking lot instead of a twenty-eight unit apartment building for homeless youth. Two years after that meeting, there are still less than ten apartment units designated for the estimated fifteen hundred homeless youths in the area. The numbers of homeless youth on the streets has increased noticeably in the intervening years, and the number of HIV-infected youths using case management services has increased four hundred percent.

As of this writing, the Youth Housing Project of the Central Community Housing Trust of Minneapolis is in a similar situation with a neighborhood business organization. Money has been raised to purchase and renovate a building for seventeen homeless youth ages sixteen to twenty-one, but the Project is encountering resistance in the business community.

Unfortunately, examples like this are common. Housing projects for the underprivileged, the mentally disadvantaged, for people living with AIDS, for those recovering from addiction, and for the homeless typically meet with fierce resistance. A term has been coined to describe this phenomenon. It is "NIMBY," or "Not In My Back Yard."

NIMBY is not necessarily a bad thing. To some degree, NIMBY indicates neighbors' concern for their neighborhood. NIMBY also forces housing providers to be responsible in housing development and building management.

However, NIMBY is a reaction which too often stems from fears which have little basis in reality. The concerns behind the NIMBY reaction must be identified, addressed, and challenged when they are not reasonable. If a neighborhood has concerns about housing homeless youths, its concerns should be recognized and addressed with information and, if needed, reasonable modifications to the transitional living program.

Communication between the youths, program administrators, and neighbors is also essential. Only when the concerns are accurately identified can real discussion ensue, and only when all the participants meet can the issues be resolved. Many housing developers are, by law, required to get neighborhood organizational support for their plans, and may not pursue development without it. However, behind some NIMBY responses can be racism, classism, ageism, or other prejudices. These too will become apparent when concerns are addressed. The responsible approach to NIMBY is to address real concerns with real facts, and expose any prejudice for what it is.

Examining and addressing the NIMBY reaction is important, but it will not resolve the lack of low-cost housing alone; the power dynamics of how housing resources are created and allocated in this country also must be altered. Currently, most low-income housing is owned by private investors or public housing authorities. Neither party has adequate incentive to serve homeless youth or preserve low-income housing. Private investors have been trying to dispose of their low-income rental properties since tax law changes in 1986 destroyed much of their investment incentive. On the other side of the aisle, public housing authorities have become paralyzed in bureaucracy while waiting lists for housing are measured in years. The government, their employer, has given them no incentive to expand services to homeless youth.

Any destruction of low-income housing in the U.S. during our current housing shortage is not unlike the withholding of food from the starving in lesser developed countries. In other words, while we have the resources desperately needed by the homeless and starving, political pressures and bureaucracy keep us from distributing them where they are most urgently needed. There need to be financial incentives created for the controlling interests to preserve the current housing stock, but until then, we need laws passed to prevent the continued destruction of low-income housing for private gain.

CONCLUSION

While talking to hundreds of people as I prepared to write this book, I developed the impression that important social research has been neglected. When the number of older unaccompanied youths began to increase dramatically in the 1980s, we did not stop to investigate the causes or the needs and the wants of this population. Instead, we just provided them more of the same care we had given to the earlier youths, who had generally been more compliant and troubled. We have neglected to study any changes in the population, or the basic dynamics of providing support.

In another sense, we have never acknowledged that homeless youths are the customers, and that different forms of institutionalized care are the products. We never acknowledged that youths have the power to choose. That government programs are not the only sources of care which can be chosen by street kids. Competing with the various programs and institutions for the chance to "provide for" homeless youth are gangs, pimps, and street families. Our mistaken assumptions and poor understanding of homeless kids did not allow us to think for an instant that they might choose the alternatives.

Choosing unsafe and uncomfortable alternatives to social welfare programs can (at least in the short term) preserve a sense of independence and freedom. And for homeless youth, the short term is all that exists. Instead of listening to the youths before expanding our programs, we listened to the professionals who were invested in the preservation and growth of their respective care organizations as they told us how youths needed treatment. Their answer was more foster care, more group homes—more of the same. No one talked to the youths. With this in mind, is it surprising that we now have overbuilt, outdated, and ineffective care and treatment institutions from which youths run away?

The "Father Knows Best" attitude towards providing care may work for younger kids who see no alternatives and who can't recognize mistreatment, but for older youths who are without the basic necessities of life and have learned to live out on the streets, we can be authoritarian no longer. Society has neglected to provide basic life support for these youth, and it has lost their respect. They will not listen to us because we have not listened to them.

In any service organization, the client needs to be at the center of program design. Homeless youths need to be brought into board meetings and program planning sessions and heard. Follow up must be done on past clients, and their critiques and evaluations of the programs must be solicited. Given an ear, homeless youths will display their humanity, and they will often critique a program with profound insight. Most importantly, they will describe their foremost needs for basic necessities and will expound on their hopes and plans to achieve independence.

I am not suggesting that homeless youths are aware of all that is necessary regarding their care. I am not saying that older adolescents will always recognize the value of education, or that they are experts on their own mental health. But instead of attempting to direct their future, we can assist them most effectively by working with them to achieve their goals, showing them the steps along the way and outlining an effective and realistic plan with them. Like the rest of us, homeless youths will always have things to learn about the process of realizing goals. It is here we can best help.

In many senses of the word, these youths are adults. They have seen too much to be innocent; they have provided for themselves for too long. As best they can be, they are independent, and have taken charge of their lives. We need to recognize their experiences and acknowledge the adult responsibilities they have assumed while we help them achieve healthy self-sufficiency. To expect them to be children again by giving up their adult freedoms and responsibilities, by returning to foster homes or other institutionalized child care, is to fail to understand them. Our continued view of them as either helpless children or predatory criminals is the crux of misunderstanding between homeless youth and our society.